MACHETE SEASON

MACHETE SEASON

THE KILLERS IN RWANDA SPEAK

A REPORT BY

JEAN HATZFELD

TRANSLATED FROM THE FRENCH BY

LINDA COVERDALE

PREFACE BY

SUSAN SONTAG

FARRAR, STRAUS AND GIROUX / NEW YORK

FARRAR, STRAUS AND GIROUX
19 Union Square West, New York 10003

Copyright © 2003 by Éditions du Seuil
Translation copyright © 2005 by Farrar, Straus and Giroux, LLC
Preface copyright © 2005 by Susan Sontag
All rights reserved
Distributed in Canada by Douglas & McIntyre Ltd.
Printed in the United States of America
Originally published in 2003 by Éditions du Seuil, France,
as Une saison de machettes
Published in the United States by Farrar, Straus and Giroux
First American edition, 2005

This book is published with the assistance of the French Ministry
of Culture–National Book Center.

Library of Congress Cataloging-in-Publication Data
Hatzfeld, Jean.
    [Saison de machettes. English]
    Machete season : the killers in Rwanda speak : a report / by Jean
Hatzfeld ; preface by Susan Sontag ; translated from the French by
Linda Coverdale.
        p. cm.
    ISBN-13: 978-0-374-28082-6
    ISBN-10: 0-374-28082-7 (alk. paper)
    1. Rwanda—History—Civil War, 1994– —Atrocities.
2. Rwanda—History—Civil War, 1994– —Personal narratives.
3. Tutsi (African people)—Crimes against—Rwanda—History—
20th century.   4. Hutu (African people)—Rwanda.   5. Genocide—
Rwanda—History—20th century.   6. Rwanda—Ethnic relations—
History—20th century.   I. Title.

DT450.435.H3914 2005
967.57104′31—dc22

                                                            2004061600

Designed by Gretchen Achilles

www.fsgbooks.com

1   3   5   7   9   10   8   6   4   2

CONTENTS

PREFACE

Ours is, appallingly, an age of genocide, but even so, what happened in Rwanda in the spring of 1994 stands out in several ways. In a tiny, landlocked African country smaller than the state of Maryland, some 800,000 people were hacked to death, one by one, by their neighbors. The women, men, and children who were slaughtered were of the same race and shared the same language, customs, and confession (Roman Catholic) as those who eagerly slaughtered them.

"It's too difficult to judge us," says one of the perpetrators of the Rwandan genocide who agreed to describe to Jean Hatzfeld what he had done. Why? "Because what we did goes beyond human imagination." But that is just the point. Yes, what was done in Rwanda goes beyond human imagination, and yes, human beings, hundreds of thousands of otherwise normal people, not professional killers, did it. Against the constant backdrop of reflection about the Shoah and other modern genocides, Hatzfeld has harvested a unique set of avowals that forces us to confront the unthinkable, the unimaginable. This is not courtroom testimony but a series of remarkably varied reflections by articulate people who do, in large measure, understand what they have done and still hope to be forgiven and to get on with their lives.

Our obligation, and it is an obligation, is to take in what human beings are capable of doing to one another, not spontaneously (crimes of this order are never spontaneous) but when mobilized to think of other human beings—people who were their school friends, neighbors, co-workers, and fellow parishioners—as not human beings at all, and when organized for and directed to the task of slaughter. For the issue, finally, is not judgment. It is understanding. To make the effort to understand what happened in Rwanda is a painful task that we have no right to shirk—it is part of being a moral adult. Everyone should read Hatzfeld's book.

SUSAN SONTAG

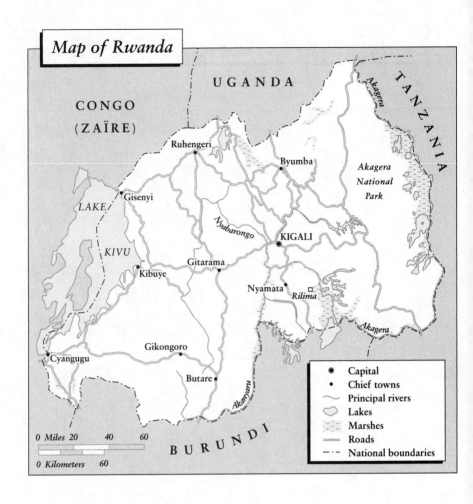

Map of Rwanda

CONGO
(ZAÏRE)

UGANDA

TANZANIA

Ruhengeri

Byumba

Akagera

Akagera
National
Park

LAKE
Gisenyi

KIVU

Nyabarongo

KIGALI

Kibuye

Gitarama

Nyamata

Rilima

Cyangugu

Gikongoro

Butare

Akanyaru

Akagera

BURUNDI

● Capital
● Chief towns
〜 Principal rivers
🗺 Lakes
▦ Marshes
═ Roads
–·– National boundaries

0 Miles 20   40   60

0 Kilometers   60

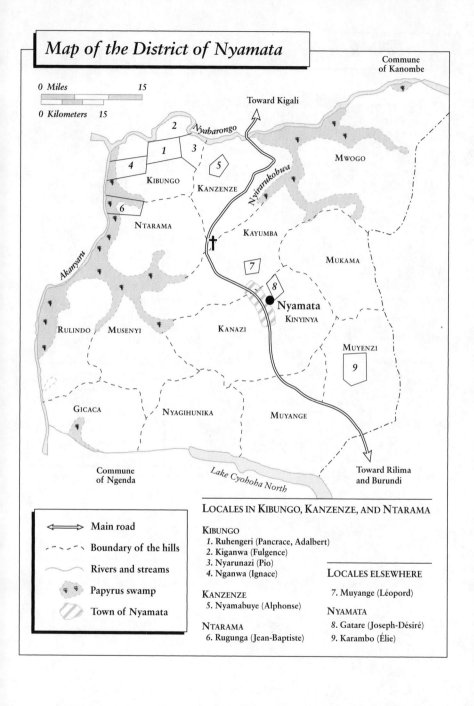

Map of the District of Nyamata

0 Miles   15

0 Kilometers   15

Commune
of Kanombe

Toward Kigali

Nyabarongo

2

1

3

4

KIBUNGO

5

KANZENZE

MWOGO

Nyirarukobwa

6

NTARAMA

Akanyaru

KAYUMBA

MUKAMA

7

8

Nyamata

KINYINYA

RULINDO   MUSENYI

KANAZI

MUYENZI

9

GICACA   NYAGIHUNIKA

MUYANGE

Commune
of Ngenda

Lake Cyohoha North

Toward Rilima
and Burundi

⟸⟹ Main road

- - - - Boundary of the hills

~~~~ Rivers and streams

Papyrus swamp

Town of Nyamata

LOCALES IN KIBUNGO, KANZENZE, AND NTARAMA

KIBUNGO
1. Ruhengeri (Pancrace, Adalbert)
2. Kiganwa (Fulgence)
3. Nyarunazi (Pio)
4. Nganwa (Ignace)

KANZENZE
5. Nyamabuye (Alphonse)

NTARAMA
6. Rugunga (Jean-Baptiste)

LOCALES ELSEWHERE

7. Muyange (Léopord)

NYAMATA
8. Gatare (Joseph-Désiré)
9. Karambo (Élie)

CHRONOLOGY OF EVENTS IN RWANDA AND ESPECIALLY IN NYAMATA

1921 Under a League of Nations mandate, Rwanda and Burundi, formerly part of German East Africa and occupied by Belgian troops during World War I, fall under Belgian rule.

1931 Identity cards specifying the ethnic group of the bearer are introduced, a policy continued until 1994.

1946 Rwanda becomes a UN trust territory and is administered as a Belgian colony and part of Congo.

1959 The last great Tutsi king, Mutara Rudahigwa, dies. The Hutu peasant massacres and revolts that follow cause the exodus of hundreds of thousands of Tutsis.

1960 The Belgian Congo becomes independent, and Rwanda becomes a republic.

1961 The Hutu parties achieve victory in Rwanda's first legislative elections.

1962 The independence of Rwanda is proclaimed.

1963 In Nyamata, the Rwandan army carries out the first widespread massacres of Tutsis.

1973 Major Juvénal Habyarimana carries out a military coup d'état. Large numbers of Hutus fleeing poverty and drought flood into Nyamata, where renewed and repeated massacres occur.

1978 Juvénal Habyarimana is elected president.

1990 The Tutsi-led Rwandan Patriotic Front, which has been assembled from Tutsi militias operating out of Tanzania, Uganda, Burundi, and Zaire, gains its first military victories in Rwanda. Hutu extremist militias, called *interahamwe*, are organized by the Habyarimana clan.

1993 A peace agreement is signed in Arusha, Tanzania, between Habyarimana's regime and the RPF.

1994
April 6, 8 p.m. Habyarimana is assassinated when his plane is brought down by a mysterious missile on its approach to Kigali Airport.
April 7, early morning. Assassinations begin of political figures who did not fully support Habyarimana's dictatorship; the victims include Prime Minister Agathe Uwilingiyamana, a Hutu.

RPF forces immediately begin their drive toward the capital, Kigali, where Hutu *interahamwe* militias have started slaughtering Tutsis and moderate Hutus. The genocide begins; it will continue for about a hundred days. In Nyamata, small-scale violence breaks out, definitively separating the two ethnic communities on the hills.
April 9. In Nyamata *interahamwe* troops launch the first raids to loot and burn houses abandoned by Tutsis and to murder rebellious Hutus; local farmers help them, but without receiving specific orders.

April 11. After waiting four days for directions from the government, Hutu soldiers from the base at Gako begin systematic killings in the streets of Nyamata. On the hills, the local authorities and *interahamwe* assemble the farmers, and their planned attacks on Tutsis begin.

April 14–15. In Nyamata approximately five thousand Tutsi refugees are massacred by machete, first in the church, then in the Sainte-Marthe Maternity Hospital.

April 15. Some five thousand refugees are massacred in the church in Ntarama, thirty kilometers from Nyamata.

April 16. Organized hunts for Tutsis begin in the marshes of Nyamwiza and on the hill of Kayumba—wherever Tutsis have sought refuge.

May 12. Tens of thousands of Hutu families start fleeing toward Congo on the Gitarama road. The genocide in Nyamata is over.

May 14. The RPF reaches Nyamata and begins to look for survivors in the marshes.

July 4. Kigali center falls to the RPF, which installs a new government with a Hutu president and General Paul Kagame as minister of defense. The RPF was eventually reorganized into the regular Rwandan army.

July 15. Half a million Hutu refugees begin to cross the border into Congo; eventually some 1.7 million Hutus fill the refugee camps of eastern Congo.

October 3. The United Nations Security Council endorses a report describing the massacres committed in Rwanda as genocide.

1996

November. Rebel forces opposing President Mobutu Sese Seko's regime invade eastern Congo, supported by Rwandan forces. Tens of thousands of Hutu refugees are killed, and some two million refugees eventually return to Rwanda. Most *interahamwe* either were killed during this Rwandan offensive or joined the return and gave themselves up to the Rwandan government, but some still live in Congo, in bands of looters or mercenaries, mostly in the Kivu region on the border.

1997

May 17. Troops of the Rwandan army sweep through Congo, driving out Mobutu and bringing Laurent-Désiré Kabila to power in Kinshasa.

1998

April 24. In Nyamata six condemned prisoners are publicly executed on the hill of Kayumba—to this day, the sole official executions there.

2002

January 1. The Third Republic is proclaimed in Rwanda, consolidating the regime of President Paul Kagame, who has been the strong man of the RPF from the start.

August. *Gaçaça* courts begin operating in Nyamata.

2003

January 1. A presidential decree is issued concerning those convicted of crimes of genocide. It authorizes the release of elderly and sick prisoners and allows probation—in conjunction with three days of communal labor per week—for convicts in the second and third categories (lower-echelon killers and their accomplices) whose confessions have been accepted and who have already served at least half their prison sentences.

MACHETE SEASON

EARLY MORNING

In April the nocturnal rains often leave in their wake black clouds that mask the first rays of the sun. Rose Kubwimana knows how dawn comes late on the marshes at this time of year. That faint gray glow is not what is puzzling her.

Rose is crouching barefoot near a brownish pond, her skirt hiked up across her thighs, her calloused hands resting on her knees. She is wearing a woolen sweater. Next to her lie two plastic five-liter jerry cans. She comes every morning to this pool, where the water is less muddy and the edge, thick with palm trees, is less spongy than at other ponds.

This one is hidden by fronds of *umunyeganyege*, a kind of dwarf palm; beyond lies an infinity of other ponds, puddles, and quagmires scattered among thickets of papyrus. Rose inhales the fetid and familiar odor of the marshes, a smell that seems particularly musty this morning. She also recognizes the fragrance of the white water lilies. Since her arrival, she has sensed something strange in the air, and finally she understands: it is the sounds. The sighing of the marshes does not sound normal this morning.

She hears the usual racket of the ibises, the short explosive whistles of the long-tailed *talapoin* monkeys, but only in the distance. In her immediate vicinity, the marshes have fallen silent. There is no furtive rustling of *sitatungas*, the antelopes that live in the marshes and feed on papyrus; there is no grumpy grunting of pigs to startle her; the big, green, white-crested turacos, usually such early risers in the fig trees, are not uttering their piercing and punctual *ko ko ko*; perhaps they have slipped away like the other denizens of the dawn.

Rose Kubwimana is a rather elderly lady, lean, tall, and strong. Her hair is turning gray. Her house is an hour's walk away in the forest. In the more than twenty years that she has been coming to fetch the family's water, she has never noticed this silence before, neither during the great droughts that dry up the mire nor when torrential rains flood the boggy earth. It is not heaven sent, she knows that. She is apprehensive but not really surprised.

The previous day, going down to the truck stop at the crossroads, she passed by the church in Ntarama and saw the encampment. She knows that for three days now, local Tutsi families have been gathering there. She also knows, because she has seen some of them, that many Tutsis have taken refuge down in the school at Cyugaro, or have gone all the way down to the river to hide around there, probably not far from her pond.

Later, of that morning in limbo, she will say simply: "Up in the hills, I thought terrible cuttings were brewing and life would be all torn apart. But as for the marshes, truly, I did not think the blades and chaos would come down that far. I did not think it, but I felt it." She will merely add, "From the first day time has wanted to be most secretive about these things. Me, I stand behind time's wishes for now."

That first day was April 11, 1994. On April 6, late in the evening, the President of the Republic of Rwanda, Juvénal Habyarimana, a Hutu, had been assassinated upon his return from a visit to Burundi when his plane exploded over the airport at Kigali, the capital. The massacres of the genocide began that same night in Kigali, then spread to Rwanda's provincial towns and cities, and a few days later reached the hills, as they did here, in the region of Bugesera.

Rose fills the jerry cans, settles the first one on her head, steadies it with one hand as she picks up the second can, then climbs back up the hill through tangles of brush and vines. In her courtyard of beaten earth, ocher like the fields and the walls of her house, she sees Adalbert. He has awakened earlier than usual and is smoking a cigarette, sitting on a tiny stool.

Adalbert is the brawniest of her twelve children. His impressively broad shoulders seem to send a feverish energy coursing through his arms. He is a stout worker, talkative and full of fun in the local *cabarets*.* He has not yet chosen a wife for himself. A dictatorial man, he makes all the decisions in the household. This morning he is wearing flip-flops, Bermuda shorts, a shirt, and a curious pouch at his waist, all signs that he will not be going to the fields.

Adalbert runs water over his hands, rubs his face, rinses his mouth, and spits. Last night he went to bed late, and drunk. He eats neither the sorghum porridge nor the beans heating on the embers, hardly speaks to anyone except his brother, and takes off. "He left fired up," Rose will later say.

*The Rwandan cabaret can be an authentic tavern, with a proper sign and a terrace, but is often a more humble combination of social club, bar, and general store. It might be nothing more than a few thatched huts in someone's front yard or a one-room shop with no sign, a floor of beaten earth, cases of beer and soft drinks stacked against the back wall, and bottles and large cans of banana and sorghum beer lined up behind the counter. The shop might stock rice, potatoes, beans, cooking oil, fabrics, underwear, shampoo, batteries, and so forth. A sofa, a bench, and some stools sit around a low table just inside the door for rainy weather, and if it's sunny, patrons move their seats outside.

After mornings in the fields, farmers put away their hoes and head for some socializing and refreshment, so the cabarets are busy in the afternoons. Real beer is expensive, but homebrew is available, even—for the temporarily strapped—by the swallow, through a long reed straw, from a container behind the counter. Brochettes of goat meat smoke appetizingly on grills in the back courtyard, and patrons are welcome until late in the evening. —Translator's note

The path hugs the hill: above rises the eucalyptus forest, while below, to the left, lies the marshy valley of the Nyabarongo River, where his mother drew water earlier. Adalbert doesn't notice any unusual silence—he's in too much of a hurry. When he reaches Pancrace's house, all the women and girls in the family are already at work, some in the courtyard, others in the planting fields. He exchanges a few words of welcome and friendly banter with them. Emerging bare-chested from his house, Pancrace hastens to join Adalbert.

The next stop on this path overlooking the banana groves is the home of Fulgence, who comes out in his white leather sandals. He wears them everywhere, probably because he is a part-time clergyman. Fulgence is thin, and so is his voice. He speaks briefly with Adalbert. About what? Later he will recall: "I'd found a running sore on a goat's hoof, but Adalbert told me it would just have to wait till evening."

Next comes the house of Pio, who is hardly more than a boy. Like Adalbert, he is bursting with energy, but his character is gentler. Soccer is his passion. His mother offers the youths a big can of banana beer, *urwagwa*,* and they drink it in long swallows interrupted by their thanks. When the friends set out this time, they leave the river path, turning their backs on the valley to climb among the perfumed ramparts of yellow-flowering *kimbazi* trees, making for the summit. This morning the path is not only much busier than on market days in Nyamata, but also crowded only with men.

---

*Banana beer (*urwagwa*) is three times cheaper than ordinary beer and three times as potent, which explains its huge popularity on the hills, aside from the fact that it can be delicious. Bananas are buried for three days in a pit to overripen, after which the juice is pressed out and mixed with sorghum flour, left another three days to ferment, then strained and bottled. Urwagwa is more or less strong, tart, and harsh, depending on the time of year and the brewer's expertise; when ready, it must be consumed within three days. It is drunk from a bottle with a single reed straw, which the buyer passes around to his drinking companions. During long droughts and when bananas are scarce, tipplers may fall back on ikigage, a sorghum beer that is less tasty but just as intoxicating.*

Even more excitement awaits our group up in Kibungo. The school playground is as packed as on the first day of classes, but with adults. Farther along people are strolling around the flat area where the shops are clustered, with their ochre adobe walls and corrugated metal roofs. Everyone is talking about the events of the previous day, shouting and cracking lots of jokes.

The group heads for a *cabaret*, finding seats on the low wall of the veranda. In the backyard, women hover over a fire from which rises the savory smell of grilled meat. Pancrace waves over one of the women and orders brochettes, which arrive immediately on a tin plate along with salt, peppers, and slices of banana. The group fetches bottles of Primus beer, which they uncap one against the other, eating and drinking with hearty appetites. Alphonse happens by and joins them on the wall, slapping palms with everyone and snatching up a brochette.

At the same moment, on the slope of the hill across the valley, in the village of Ntarama, Jean-Baptiste, a civil servant, steps out his front door in the pale green suit he wears to work. He gives instructions to someone through the door, which he padlocks, strangely enough, as though he were imprisoning the other person. He calls over a boy leaning against a tree in the garden, slips him a rolled-up bill, whispers more instructions, then goes off in the direction of Kibungo.

Meanwhile, thirty kilometers away, Léopord and old Élie clamber into the back of a truck driving through Nyamata. Soldiers are crisscrossing the main street, and there's a corpse lying in the marketplace. All along the unpaved road to Kibungo, the truck honks its way past an endless stream of men on foot or on bicycles.

And honking his way through Kibungo, the burgomaster's driver gives everyone the official signal to assemble on the soccer field. Adalbert and his pals finish their grilled meat, grab themselves each a bottle of beer from a case, and join the throng. On the ridge between Kibungo and Ntarama, goal posts made of eucalyptus trunks mark a clearing as the soccer field, one of the rare flat places in this landscape. Buses, army trucks, and vans pour in and park all around the field, which slowly fills with men. In the center of the field is the striking figure of Joseph-Désiré Bitero, in a khaki uniform, surrounded by thugs armed with guns.

Off to one side, Adalbert's group can't hear the ranting speeches through all the noise; they can barely recognize the orators who climb, each in turn, onto the hood of a van. As they drain their beer bottles, which they toss into the grass, the friends call greetings to this or that acquaintance, chatting in particular with Ignace, who has been looking for them. When the crowd surges forward, Adalbert signals to everyone to stay together and follow him as they move off on a path leading through the forest toward the hamlet of Nyarunazi.

Most of the houses seem already abandoned. The group finds Célestin, a well-known local healer, on his front porch. He brings them a fresh plate of brochettes and a big can of banana beer with one straw, which they all pass around, but he begs off going with them because he has business to attend to. His age and the can of *urwagwa* argue in his favor, and the group sets out again.

Whistles and gunshots ring out in the distance. The friends don't join the main body of men, who are already searching fields and the surrounding bush. Pancrace will later say, "We knew that it was wasted effort, that our chief task probably waited for us lower down." Familiar with the marshes, and suspecting that Tutsis have already gone to ground deep in the swamps, they are the first Hutus to arrive there. A pounding cloudburst sweeps the mist from the horizon, suddenly revealing papyrus bogs that stretch as far as the eye can see. Without the slightest hesitation, the young men leave dry land and plunge up to their knees in the muck, pushing the foliage aside with one hand, gripping their machetes in the other.

In April 2000 I wrote a book presenting narratives by survivors of the Rwandan genocide in this very commune of Nyamata, *Dans le nu de la vie: Récits des marais rwandais* (Into the Quick of Life: Stories from the Rwandan Marshes). It opened with this sentence: "In 1994, between eleven in the morning on Monday April 11 and two in the afternoon on Saturday May 14, about fifty thousand Tutsis, out of a population of around fifty-nine thousand, were massacred by machete, murdered every day of the week, from nine-thirty in the morning until four in the afternoon, by Hutu neighbors and militiamen, on the hills of the commune of Nyamata, in Rwanda. That is the point of departure of this book."

It is the point of departure of this book as well, except that this one deals with the men from whom those survivors escaped, the killers who murdered their Tutsi neighbors. I focus in particular on killers who lived on the three hills—Kibungo, Ntarama, and Kanzenze—bordering the Nyamwiza marshes.

HOW IT WAS ORGANIZED

PANCRACE:★ During that killing season we rose earlier than usual, to eat lots of meat, and we went up to the soccer field at around nine or ten o'clock. The leaders would grumble about latecomers, and we would go off on the attack. Rule number one was to kill. There was no rule number two. It was an organization without complications.

PIO: We would wake up at six o'clock. We ate brochettes of grilled meat and nourishing food because of all the running we had to do. We met up in town, near the shops, and chatted with pals along the way to the soccer field. There they would give us orders about the killings and our itineraries for the day, and off we went, beating the bush, working our way down to the marshes. We formed a line to wade into the mud and the papyrus. Then we broke up into small bands of friends or acquaintances.

We got on fine, except for the days when there was a huge fuss, when *interahamwe*† reinforcements came in from the surrounding areas in motor vehicles to lead the bigger operations. Because those young hotheads ran us ragged on the job.

FULGENCE: On April 11 the municipal judge in Kibungo sent his messengers to gather the Hutus up there. Lots of *interahamwe* had

★ *The names of the killers are differentiated from those of other speakers by capital letters.*
† *"Those who attack together": the Hutu extremist militias created by the Habyarimana clan in the early 1990s, trained by the Rwandan army and sometimes, locally, by French soldiers.*

arrived in trucks and buses, all jostling and honking on the roads. It was like a city traffic jam.

The judge told everyone there that from then on we were to do nothing but kill Tutsis. Well, we understood: that was a final plan. The atmosphere had changed.

That day misinformed guys had come to the meeting without bringing a machete or some other cutting tool. The *interahamwe* lectured them: they said it would pass this once but had better not happen twice. They told them to arm themselves with branches and stones, to form barriers at the rear to cut off any escaping fugitives. Afterward everyone wound up a leader or a follower, but nobody ever forgot his machete again.

PANCRACE: The first day, a messenger from the municipal judge went house to house summoning us to a meeting right away. There the judge announced that the reason for the meeting was the killing of every Tutsi without exception. It was simply said, and it was simple to understand.

So the only questions were about the details of the operation. For example, how and when we had to begin, since we were not used to this activity, and where to begin, too, since the Tutsis had run off in all directions. There were even some guys who asked if there were any priorities. The judge answered sternly: "There is no need to ask how to begin. The only worthwhile plan is to start straight ahead into the bush, and right now, without hanging back anymore behind questions."

ADALBERT: We sorted ourselves out on the soccer field. This team went up, that team went down, another team set out for a different swamp. The lucky ones could look around for chances to loot. At first the burgomaster, the subprefect, and the municipal councilors were coordinating all that, along with the soldiers or retired policemen, thanks to their guns. In any case, if you owned a weapon, even an old grenade, you were pushed forward and found yourself in favor.

Later on the bravest young guys became leaders, the ones who gave orders without hesitation and strode eagerly along. Me, I made myself the leader for all the residents of Kibungo from the very first day. Previously I was leader of the church choir, so now I became a real leader, so to speak. The residents approved me without a hitch.

We liked being in our gang. We all agreed about the new activities, we decided on the spot where we would go to work, we helped one another out like comrades. If someone presented a little excuse, we would offer to take on his part of the job that one time. The organization was a bit casual, but it was respected and conscientious.

ALPHONSE: We would wake up, wash, eat, relieve ourselves, call to our neighbors, and go off in small scouting parties. We did not change our morning routines, except for the wake-up time, which could be earlier or later, depending on the events of the day before.

For breakfast, there was nothing fancy. Usually we ate what our wives prepared—a big meal, obviously. In the evening, it depended on how the day had gone. If many reinforcements from the neighboring hills had turned up, the leaders took advantage of having these attackers along to bring off more profitable hunting expeditions, surrounding the fugitives on all sides. It was double work, in a way. And in the evening, we had to gather again in town to eat meat together, show some friendship to the *interahamwe*, get on an easy footing with our colleagues from away, listen to the authorities' announcements, and share the spoils.

But on days of ordinary expeditions, we did not hang out that long at the marketplace *cabaret*, preferring to go home early or pop a Primus with buddies. We took advantage of these lulls to get some rest and quiet time.

The more reinforcements there were, the farther into the marshes the expeditions had to push, the more papyrus we had to plow through, the longer we had to race through the muck, machetes in hand, and the more tired we came home. All sweaty and dripping with slime. The outside reinforcements and their enthusiasm—that was the toughest pressure the organization put on us.

IGNACE: We'd gather in a crowd of about a thousand on the soccer field, head out into the bush along with one or two hundred hunters, all led by two or three gentlemen with guns, soldiers or intimidators. At the muddy edge of the first clumps of papyrus, we separated into teams of acquaintances.

Those who wanted to chat, chatted. Those who wanted to dawdle, dawdled—if they could avoid being noticed. Those who wanted to sing, sang. We didn't choose special songs to raise our spirits, no patriotic airs like the ones on the radio, no mean or mocking words about the Tutsis. We didn't need encouraging verses, we just naturally turned to traditional songs we liked. So we were marching choirs.

In the bogs, you had to hunt and kill only up till the last whistle. Sometimes a gunshot replaced the whistle—that would be the sole surprise of the day.

ÉLIE: The intimidators made the plans and whipped up enthusiasm; the shopkeepers paid and provided transportation; the farmers prowled and pillaged. For the killings, though, everybody had to show up blade in hand and pitch in for a decent stretch of work.

People would bristle only when the leaders announced compulsory collections of money to pay the men who went to help out in neighboring sectors. Folks grumbled especially about collections organized to give bonuses to *interahamwe* from nearby areas.

As for us, we frowned on those big operations, finding it more profitable for everyone to stick to his own backyard. We knew those who came long distances expected large rewards. Deep down, we didn't like them; we preferred handling things ourselves.

Concerning the business of the killings and compensations, people from the different hills did not have a sharing turn of mind.

LÉOPORD: I was the junior official in charge of killing for the unit in Muyange. It was something new for me, of course. So I got up earlier than those around me to review the preparations. I would whistle for assembly, hurry along the laggards, scold the slugabeds, count up the missing, check on the reasons for absence, and pass on the instructions. If a meeting of organizers produced a reprimand or an announcement, I delivered it directly. I gave the signal to set out.

The people of Kibungo, Kanzenze, and Ntarama would gather on the Kibungo soccer field. The people of Muyange and Karambo assembled in front of the Pentecostal church of Maranyundo. If there were brochettes there, we ate. If there were orders, we listened and got going.

Usually we had to go through the bush on foot—that is why we got up earlier than our colleagues in Kibungo. During that time, however, there were many vehicles on the road. The drivers were obliging and offered free rides in the backs of their trucks, and certain merchants increased the giveaway round-trips, so you could find a spot in a commercial van or an army bus. It depended on your rank or your luck.

ÉLIE: We had to work fast, and we got no time off, especially not Sundays—we had to finish up. We canceled all ceremonies. Everyone was hired at the same level for a single job—to crush all the cockroaches. The intimidators gave us only one objective and only one way to achieve it. Anyone who detected something irregular, he brought it up quietly; anyone needing a dispensation, the same. I don't know how it was organized in other regions— in ours it was rudimentary.

JEAN-BAPTISTE: When you get right down to it, it is a gross exaggeration to say we organized ourselves up on the hills. The plane came down April 6. A very small number of local Hutus went straight for retaliation. But most waited four days in their houses and in the nearest *cabarets*, listening to the radio, watching Tutsis flee, chatting and joking without planning a thing.

On April 10 the burgomaster in a pressed suit and all the authorities gathered us together. They lectured us, they threatened in advance anyone who bungled the job, and the killings began without much planning. The only regulation was to keep going till the end, maintain a satisfactory pace, spare no one, and loot what we found. It was impossible to screw up.

IGNACE: After the plane crash, we no longer worried about who had followed the teachings of the presidential party or the teachings of a rival party. We forgot all quarrels, and who had fallen out with whom in the past. We kept only one idea in the pot.

We no longer asked who had trained with guns and gained useful knowhow in a militia, or whose hands had never left a hoe. We had work to do, and we were doing our best. We didn't care one way or the other who preferred to take his orders from the burgomaster, the *interahamwe*, or our well-known municipal judge. We obeyed on all sides, and we found satisfaction in that.

Suddenly Hutus of every kind were patriotic brothers without any partisan discord. We were through playing around with political words. We were no longer in our each-to-his-own mood. We were doing a job to order. We were lining up behind everyone's enthusiasm. We gathered into teams on the soccer field and went out hunting as kindred spirits.

THE THREE HILLS

ying languidly beneath carpets of papyrus, reeds, and water lilies, two wide rivers and a lake mark the boundaries of the Bugesera region: on the west is the Akanyaru River; on the north and, after a bend, east, the Nyabarongo River; on the south, Lake Cyohoha. In the past, a lake called Cyohoha North cut across the region, but it has succumbed to recent dry spells, the local effects of El Niño. A rutted, unpaved road runs the length of the Bugesera, linking Kigali to the north and the border of Burundi to the south—a trip that takes five or six hours by minibus, travel uncushioned by shock absorbers, which one by one give way beneath the overload of passengers.

Although the Bugesera is surrounded by marshes and enjoys two rainy seasons a year, its arid soil of ocher laterite has long discouraged settlement. Natural sources of drinking water are in fact quite rare in this landscape of dust and clay.

Entering the Bugesera via the bridge across the Nyabarongo, one finds the first trickle of pure water twenty-five kilometers into the interior. Far from the putrid marshes, this stream of groundwater is the Rwaki-Birizi, which supplies Nyamata. Year in and year out, well before the first light of dawn, a mob—of women and girls with a jerry can in one hand and another on their heads, and boys with pedicabs rigged up to carry three or four cans—besieges the spring at Rwaki-Birizi, seeking water for their own households and those of their employers or clients.

. . .

Immigration into the Bugesera dates back to 1959, when Mutara Rudahigwa, the last great Tutsi king, or *mwami*, died, after which the Hutus rose in a murderous rebellion. Desperate Tutsis, fleeing the deadly pogroms celebrating the abolition of their monarchy, were herded onto the wooden beds of trucks provided by the Belgian colonial administration and, after traveling all night, were abandoned on the banks of the Akanyaru River.

Crossing the river, they entered a region of bush and forests, sparsely populated by modest communities of Twa pygmies and Hutu or Tutsi farmers who had lived in those hills since time immemorial, too isolated and threatened by wild animals to worry about anyone's ethnic origins. Some Tutsi elders still recall their encampments of leaf huts, protected at night by campfires, on a savanna ruled by herds of elephants and buffalo.

Innocent Rwililiza, a teacher, remembers that more recently, during the 1980s, he would sometimes see a lion, a panther, or a python through the trees along the path he took every week with the other boarders at the teachers' training college in Rilima. Such animals have been gradually pushed back toward the mountains of Akagera National Park or driven off by hunters' spears and arrows—weapons that were to reappear during the carnage of the genocide.

Dumped on the outskirts of marshes humming with mosquitoes and tsetse flies, the Tutsi pioneers encountered sleeping sickness, malaria, and typhoid. They settled in the neighborhood of the freshwater spring, clearing first those areas suitable for Ankole* cattle, and they developed the village of Nyamata,

*A cow of medium size, slender and sinewy, distinguished by splendid lyre-shaped horns and a small cervical hump similar to that of Indian cattle. Its coat is often beige or brindled gray, black, and white. Breeding Ankole cattle is the proud prerogative of the Tutsis, who raise them as a repository and sign of wealth rather than for human consumption. The communal herds that were almost wiped out in 1994, either slaughtered or rounded up and driven to Congo, have rebounded to their pre-1994 numbers.

which grew up around a church and a government office building of brick. Successive waves of Tutsis and Hutus arrived, driven from their native regions by massacres or poverty, settling in turn on the fourteen hills of Nyamata Commune.

At the beginning of the 1970s a famine raging in the fields near Gitarama drove a colony of Hutus around the mountains of Mugina to the confluence of the Akanyaru and the Nyabarongo. To avoid following in the footsteps of their Tutsi compatriots, the families pushed on across the boggy papyrus plain until they reached a virgin forest covering three hills. The hill of Ntarama bordered the Akanyaru; the hill of Kibungo lay along both rivers at the confluence; and the hill of Kanzenze faced the Nyabarongo to the north.

After Rwanda's independence was declared in 1962, local administrations throughout the country were placed in the hands of elected or appointed Hutu officials, and the Hutu settlers of the Bugesera were given free rein to claim plots of land in the forest. The new arrivals sheltered in huts and, with much hard labor, cleared the bush down to the riverbanks. These gifted farmers uncovered fertile alluvial soil particularly suited to the growing of bananas.

As the seasons passed, plantations took over more of the riverside and thinned out the forest above. After their first harvests, the Hutu farmers were able to build themselves frame houses with the beige tile roofs characteristic of their native region, as well as chicken coops and pens for goats or black pigs— connected and covered pens unlike the vast open-air enclosures of leafy branches used for Tutsi cattle. Even today, however, these Hutu farmers—or more often farmwives—walk two to three hours each morning down to the marshes to fetch, on their backs, cans of muddy water for cooking and housekeeping.

This late settlement of the region renders all discussion about either ethnic group's rights of priority and legitimacy simply hopeless. All these immigrants to the Bugesera arrived at almost the same time, traumatized by the ordeal of having to find new land to feed themselves.

On the eve of the genocide in 1994, the population of the Nyamata district—the small town and its fourteen surrounding hills, covering a total area of 398 square kilometers—was as high as 119,000. Among the fourteen hills, those of Kibungo, Kanzenze, and Ntarama accounted for 12,675 inhabitants in an area of 133 square kilometers. After the massacres, the population of Nyamata fell to 50,500 inhabitants and that of the three hills to 5,000. Within six weeks, about five out of every six Tutsis had been killed.

THE FIRST TIME

FULGENCE: First I cracked an old mama's skull with a club. But she was already lying almost dead on the ground, so I did not feel death at the end of my arm. I went home that evening without even thinking about it.

Next day I cut down some alive and on their feet. It was the day of the massacre at the church, so, a very special day. Because of the uproar, I remember I began to strike without seeing who it was, taking pot luck with the crowd, so to speak. Our legs were much hampered by the crush, and our elbows kept bumping.

At one point I saw a gush of blood begin before my eyes, soaking the skin and clothes of a person about to fall—even in the dim light I saw it streaming down. I sensed it came from my machete. I looked at the blade, and it was wet. I took fright and wormed my way along to get out, not looking at the person any-more. I found myself outside, anxious to go home—I had done enough. That person I had just struck—it was a mama, and I felt too sick even in the poor light to finish her off.

PANCRACE: I don't remember my first kill, because I did not iden-tify that one person in the crowd. I just happened to start by killing several without seeing their faces. I mean, I was striking, and there was screaming, but it was on all sides, so it was a mix-ture of blows and cries coming in a tangle from everyone.

Still, I do remember the first person who looked at me at the moment of the deadly blow. Now that was something. The eyes

of someone you kill are immortal, if they face you at the fatal instant. They have a terrible black color. They shake you more than
the streams of blood and the death rattles, even in a great turmoil
of dying. The eyes of the killed, for the killer, are his calamity if
he looks into them. They are the blame of the person he kills.

ALPHONSE: It was before the decision about vast total killings. A
group of Tutsis had retreated into the forest of Kintwi to resist.
We spotted them behind clumps of trees—they were standing
with stones and branches or tools. Grenades from some of our
leaders showered onto them. Then came a big to-do. The Tutsis
scattered, and we followed them. In the stampede an old man,
not so sturdy anymore, was knocked down as he ran. He fell in
front of me. I hacked him across his back with my *inkota*, a sharp
blade for slaughtering cattle—I had snatched it up that morning.

A youth next to me helped out silently with his machete, as if
the victim were his. When we heard the old man finish, my
young colleague indicated to me that he had known him for a
long time. His own house was just up the hill from the old man's.
He said he was well rid of him this way—you could see he was
pleased. Me, I knew this old man by name, but I had heard nothing unpleasant about him. That evening I told my wife everything. She knew only routine details about him, we did not
discuss it, and I went to sleep.

It had gone smoothly, with no need for me to struggle. Basically, that first time I was quite surprised by the speed of death,
and also by the softness of the blow, if I may say so. I had never
dealt out death before, never looked it in the face, never considered it. I had never tried it on a warm-blooded animal. Since
I was well off, on wedding days or Christmas I used to pay a boy
to kill the chickens behind the house—and just avoid all that
mess.

JEAN-BAPTISTE: We were on a path coming back from the marshes. Some youths searched the house of a gentleman named Ababanganyingabo. They frowned on him because this Hutu from Gisenyi was known to consort with Tutsis and might well lend them a hand. They discovered he had helped some Tutsis getaway their cows—behind his house, in a pen, I think. They surrounded the man and pinned him down helpless. Then I heard my name.

They called me out because they knew I was married to a Tutsi. The news about Ababanganyingabo's fix was spreading, people were waiting, all fired up because they had been killing. Someone said to the audience: "Jean-Baptiste, if you want to save the life of your wife Spéciose Mukandahunga, you have to cut this man right now. He is a cheater! Show us that you're not that kind." This person turned and ordered, "Bring me a blade." Me, I had chosen my wife for love of her beauty; she was tall and very considerate, she was fond of me, and I felt great pain to think of losing her.

The crowd had grown. I seized the machete, I struck a first blow. When I saw the blood bubble up, I jumped back a step. Someone blocked me from behind and shoved me forward by both elbows. I closed my eyes in the brouhaha and I delivered a second blow like the first. It was done, people approved, they were satisfied and moved away. I drew back. I went off to sit on the bench of a small *cabaret*, I picked up a drink, I never looked back in that unhappy direction. Afterward I learned that the man had kept moving for two long hours before finishing.

Later on we got used to killing without so much dodging around.

PIO: I had killed chickens but never an animal the stoutness of a man, like a goat or a cow. The first person, I finished him off in a rush, not thinking anything of it, even though he was a neighbor, quite close on my hill.

In truth, it came to me only afterward: I had taken the life of a neighbor. I mean, at the fatal instant I did not see in him what he had been before; I struck someone who was no longer either close or strange to me, who wasn't exactly ordinary anymore, I'm saying like the people you meet every day. His features were indeed similar to those of the person I knew, but nothing firmly reminded me that I had lived beside him for a long time.

I am not sure you can truly understand me. I knew him by sight, without knowing him. He was the first victim I killed; my vision and my thinking had grown clouded.

ÉLIE: As a retired soldier, I had already killed two civilians during some protest agitation in 1992. The first one was a social worker from the Kanazi area. She was of pleasant reputation and modest renown. I shot an arrow wildly and hit her. I saw her fall, though I did not hear her cries because of the great distance between us. I about-faced and strode off in the opposite direction, seeing nothing of her last moments. Subsequently, I was penalized with a fine. I also heard distant admonitions from her family and threats of jail, but met with no troublesome consequences.

In 1994, during the killings in the marshes, I thought myself very lucky because I could use my former army gun. It's one of our military traditions, to let a noncommissioned officer keep his weapon at the end of his career. Killing with a gun is a game compared to the machete, it's not so close up.

ADALBERT: The first day, I did not bother to kill directly, because at the start my work was to shout orders and encouragement to the team. I was the boss. Here and there I threw a grenade into the tumult on the other side, but without experiencing the effects of death, except for the shrieks.

The first person I killed with a machete, I don't remember the precise details. I was helping out at the church. I laid on big blows, I struck home on all sides, I felt the strain of effort but not of death—there was no personal pain in the commotion. Therefore the true first time worth telling from a lasting memory, for me, is when I killed two children, April 17.

That morning we were roaming around, looking to rout out Tutsis who might be hidden on plots of land in Rugazi. I came upon two children sitting in the corner of a house. They were keeping quiet as mice. I asked them to come out; they stood up, they wanted to show they were being good. I had them walk at the head of our group, to bring them back to the village square in Nyarunazi. It was time to go home, so my men and I set out, talking about our day.

As leader, I had recently been given a gun, besides the grenades. Walking along, without thinking, I decided to try it out. I put the two children side by side twenty meters away, I stood still, I shot twice at their backs. It was the first time in my life I had used a gun, because hunting is no longer customary in the Bugesera since the wild animals disappeared. For me, it was strange to see the children drop without a sound. It was almost pleasantly easy.

I walked on without bending over to check that they were really dead. I don't even know if they were moved to a more suitable place and covered up.

Now, too often, I am seized by the memory of those children, shot straight out, like a joke.

IGNACE: We were scouring a field when someone shouted that a small troop of Tutsis was hiding in the black tinstone mines of

Birombe, abandoned mines on the hill of Rusekera. The Tutsis' trickery made us angry, and we went immediately on a raid and surrounded them. Those with grenades started throwing them at the Tutsis, to scatter them, but some had hidden inside the tunnels.

We knew it took thirty minutes to get to the end of the main gallery and back. It was too chancy in the darkness filled with those dangerous Tutsis. So we hacked up bushes and woodwork from deserted houses, blocked the gallery with this firewood, and lit the pile. The Tutsis died of smoke or burns, twenty-seven in number. It was April 22, I remember perfectly. It was my first deadly expedition and the most regrettable, because of the nastiness of the burns.

LÉOPORD: Since that morning people had begun getting up the courage to kill in the streets. You could hear gunshots on the summit of Kayumba hill: it was soldiers, driving a group of fugitives back toward the parish★ and church of Nyamata. This told us that the day would heat up. I took my machete, left the house, and went to the center of town. On this side and that, people were already giving chase.

At the marketplace I saw a man running toward me. He was coming down from Kayumba, all breathless and scared, looking only for escape, and he didn't see me. I was heading up, and in passing, I gave him a machete blow at neck level, on the vulnerable vein. It came to me naturally, without thinking. Aiming was simple, since the gentleman did not fight back. He made no defensive move—he fell without shouting, without moaning. I felt nothing, just let him lie. I looked around; killing was going on every which way. I kept chasing after runaways all day long.

★ *The cluster of buildings—schools, clinics, hospitals, residences—around a church.* —Translator's note

It was sweaty-hard and stimulating, like an unforeseen diversion. I did not even keep count. Not during the action, not afterward, since I knew it would be starting up again. I cannot tell you, sincerely, how many I killed, because I forgot some along the way.

This gentleman I killed at the marketplace, I can tell you the exact memory of it because he was the first. For others, it's murky—I cannot keep track anymore in my memory. I considered them unimportant; at the time of those murders I didn't even notice the tiny thing that would change me into a killer.

A GANG

In 1970, when Ignace Rukiramacumu was thirty-seven years old, he and his family arrived in the first Hutu column that crossed the marshes to settle in the heart of the Nganwa forest, which lies along the Akanyaru River. Ignace had been twenty-six at the death of Mwami Mutara Rudahigwa, the last great Tutsi ruler, so he was quite familiar with life under the monarchy, and before the genocide he played the role of an embittered elder among his group of friends, preserving a kind of rancid memory of the bad times.

The families of Adalbert Munzigura, Fulgence Bunani, Pio Mutungirehe, and Pancrace Hakizamungili arrived soon thereafter to live in the forest of Kiganwa, which also borders the Akanyaru. Alphonse Hitiyaremye came later, starting out as a day laborer for prosperous Tutsi cattle breeders. Eventually he acquired and cleared a plot of land in the Nyamabuye forest, which lies closer to the Nyabarongo River.

Adalbert, Fulgence, Pio, Pancrace, and most of the others grew up belonging to a pack of kids who were always together. In school they naturally associated with Tutsis their own age. They hadn't lived under the former regime and were taught almost nothing about the history of Rwanda.

As adolescents, they quit school to join their elders in the fields, where they slaved all day long. Everyone, including their enemies, agrees that they were talented farmers. They went more or less religiously to church and got together for the major traditional ceremonies—marriages and funerals. Above all, they met every day at the end of the afternoon to drink *urwagwa* or, on holidays, to share some Primus and brochettes. Their favorite *cabaret* was in Nyarunazi, the hamlet closest to their hillside, but they readily uncorked a can of homebrew at someone's house or walked all the way to the lively *cabarets* at the shopping area in Kibungo.

So the pack of kids became a close-knit gang of pals. They were joined by Alphonse and occasionally by the healer Célestin Mutungirehe, Jean-Baptiste Murangira, who lived in Rugunga on Ntarama hill, and a few other youths.

Léopord Twagirayezu was close to Adalbert and Pio thanks to soccer; he was similarly athletic, and very tall. His family's land was over in Muyange, however, about twenty kilometers from the rivers, so he joined the gang less frequently, turning up to play in soccer matches, hang around the marketplace, or attend weddings.

Like Ignace Rukiramacumu, Élie Mizinge belongs to the previous generation. He became acquainted with the gang during the 1994 massacres and the subsequent flight of Hutus into exile in the Democratic Republic of Congo, and he was truly accepted as one of them during their imprisonment. Élie and Ignace are the two senior members of the gang. Their characters, however, are almost completely dissimilar. Élie formerly enjoyed many privileges, first as a soldier, then as a policeman, and he has been deeply shaken by his fate. The genocide and its aftermath have marked him: he walks hesitantly, with a stoop. Querulous, docile, almost obsequious, he nevertheless makes a real effort to understand his predicament and to show that he was overwhelmed by events and acted badly.

Ignace also knows that he went completely wrong, and he

broods out loud over his failure without making clear whether it's the undertaking itself or its outcome that he most deplores. He is one of the wiliest prisoners we interview. He'll take one step forward, two steps back, then go in the opposite direction the next day. Sometimes he affects a complete indifference to others or stares at us accusingly, uttering bizarre prophecies.

As one of Nyamata's select group of leading citizens, Joseph-Désiré Bitero did not belong to the gang but became friends with a few of its members in his capacity as municipal chief of the *interahamwe*. He grew particularly close to Adalbert and Léopord, the two dynamic activists, and Élie, the retired policeman, whom he consulted before and during the killings.

The family of Jean Ndayambaje came from Gitarama in the same wave of immigration as Pio and Adalbert. Ten years old at the time of the genocide in 1994, Jean was too young to belong to the gang, but he worked with them after school in the neighboring fields, hung out at their local *cabaret*, and kicked the ball around on the same soccer field.

These days he does not want anything specific written about his actions during the slaughter. He speaks only of his capture by Tutsi soldiers of the Rwandan Patriotic Front★ several months after the genocide, when he was living among a horde of ragged pariahs trying to escape along the river, former *interahamwe* who were surviving by hunting and pillage; and of his incarceration at the children's detention center in Gitagata, from which he was released after three years. He was never tried on the charges brought against him, thanks to an amnesty granted to

★ *This Tutsi organization was formed on the basis of exiled troops that organized in Uganda and other neighboring nations in 1988; it began military operations against the Rwandan Army in 1990. On the opening day of the 1994 genocide against the Tutsis, it launched a vast offensive and by July 4 took definitive control of the country, under the command of Paul Kagame, who later became president of the Republic of Rwanda. The RPF was subsequently reorganized into the regular Rwandan Army, currently engaged mainly in the Congolese region of Kivu. —Translator's note* detainees who were younger than fourteen at the time of the massacres.

Today a stocky youth dressed in shorts and T-shirts acquired in prison, Jean spends every possible moment, from dawn to dusk, sweating over the family fields in Kibungo. He turns a distrustful eye and an enigmatic smile, which can turn sly or disillusioned, upon all his fellow men, and he no longer wishes to be involved in the affairs of the world, apart from swigging a bottle of banana beer on Saturday nights.

Clémentine Murebwayre has no ties with this gang beyond the fact that she lives in an adobe house on the hill of Kibungo. She is about thirty years old, with tiny brown freckles that make her delicate features even more lovely. She is Hutu, born in town; an uncle was the go-between for her marriage to Jean-de-Dieu Ruzindana, a Tutsi and "a very good man despite the drawbacks of the countryside, who had settled me in nicely with his family in Kibungo." Clémentine and her husband had nothing in common with the members of the gang and did not patronize the same *cabaret* but knew them well because their plot of land lay next to those of Pancrace and Adalbert.

Clémentine remembers: "That bunch was famous on the hill for their carousing and tomfoolery. Those fellows did not seem so bad, except maybe old Ignace, grousing all his days against the Tutsis. But when they had been drinking, they took sport in spreading misunderstandings and wicked words from *cabaret* to *cabaret*. They used to scoff at the Tutsis and promise them serious retaliation, although they never laid hands on them. They were led on by Adalbert, the strongest, the most daring, the biggest mischief-maker, always ready to pick a bone over nothing. He could bait anyone without ever losing his temper. Among ourselves, we felt that gang was growing dangersome."

Innocent Rwililiza, a survivor, also a native of Kibungo, agrees: "Those folks were hardworking, experienced farmers who could be very nice and very helpful. Still, they gradually absorbed the anti-Tutsi frustration and jealousy their parents had brought with them from Gitarama. During the killings of 1992, they suddenly fired themselves up against the Tutsis and turned very threatening. Those brawls ended without consequences in the neighborhood, thanks to the wisdom of the municipal judge. Afterward we sensed that cruelty had hooked them and could make them go wrong at any time. They seemed more and more hostile, on edge, especially whenever we had news about the war of the Tutsi *inkotanyi*.★ Yet never did we think they might one day kill at such a great pace."

During the period of our conversations, the men in the gang were all still locked up in the penitentiary at Rilima. Joseph-Désiré could not leave the section for those condemned to death, but the others gathered at dawn in the common courtyard to go about their compulsory or voluntary activities together: water chores, meals, games. Adalbert, formerly *interahamwe* chief of Kibungo and now security captain for their block, preserved his aura intact and showed all his authority during their trial. Still shod in white, Fulgence cultivated his piety. Pio maintained his good humor. Élie played the scapegoat on occasion, while Ignace continued his role as bellyacher.

Léopord no longer tried to rival Adalbert. He displayed an equal self-assurance but stayed in the background. To this day he is the only one who in a certain sense broke down. It happened in a Congolese refugee camp, where he was still acting as an *inter-*

★ *"Invincible"*: the name given to the Tutsi rebels who organized in Uganda in 1988 and fought against Habyarimana's dictatorship. They formed the basis of the Rwandan Patriotic Front.

ahamwe. Leaving an open-air mass one day, he felt the need to tell everything, to denounce himself to an astounded audience of accomplices and other *interahamwe*, who told him he'd gone crazy. Undaunted, upon his return to Nyamata he promptly offered to spill the whole story to the judges investigating his case. He is therefore one who plied his machete quite vigorously and also one whose confession is quite precise, with regard to both his own actions and those of his superiors.

Jean-Baptiste, too, decided to surrender to the tribunal and volunteer a confession immediately after his return from exile in 1996. His cooperation earned him the good will of the administration in prison, where he runs an association of repentant detainees. Jean-Baptiste—whom Innocent has called "as evil and cocky as he is crafty and intelligent"—is quite articulate but is more calculating than Léopord. He seems mealy-mouthed and evasive, although whether from cowardice or embarrassment is impossible to tell. He is in fact the one who has most clearly realized what they all did, and the one who best understands the nature of the gaze that the outside world, in Rwanda and abroad, now turns on them.

After years of silence, as their trial approached, most of the members of the gang began to admit—more or less, and with extreme caution—their participation in the genocide. They were prompted by the legal system's promises of leniency, prompted as well by the desire to preserve the gang and stay part of it. Their long-standing friendship was very important to them, they explained.

PANCRACE: In the prison meetings, friction has in a way distanced those who don't want to admit anything. Those who won't say a bit about what happened—they have to stick together and not mix anymore with those they threaten and accuse.

But among those who agree to confess, even a little, like us in the gang, friendship is as strong as before the killings.

PIO: In prison the beds of the guys in the gang are not side by side, but the daytime reunites us and helps us exchange thoughts and affection. The bygone days bound us tightly together. Especially the banana farms—we all went from one to another for the pruning and the harvests. We pressed fruit together. We invited one another to share *urwagwa*. Those who weren't so flush were included. We'd visit one who'd lost a relative to death, sharing sorrow and drink with him. We haven't forgotten those good times. That's why prison life keeps us close like before.

LÉOPORD: In the gang, we are not all open with one another in the same way, but we talk together in friendship, despite some disagreements. We help one another. We don't have drinks or little things, but we share salt or sugar, we tell jokes among ourselves to keep from getting homesick, we play volleyball and indoor games without bickering.

JEAN-BAPTISTE: There's no wrangling in the group. There are the older guys, there are the young ones—fate has not loosened our ties. Me, I try to give courage to confessions. Still, each one makes his own to suit himself. Despite the awful work of the killings and the rough prison life, the atmosphere among us remains strong. We are impatient together for an end to our difficult times. Our bad luck—I see only that as a problem for us.

ADALBERT: We avoid talking about misfortunes, like our memories of the camps or the hardships there. We form choral groups and play games. We try to protect ourselves from epidemics. We share our provisions and news of our farms, if luck allows a relative to visit the prison. We have always remained friends, always been united the same way despite the calamities of life, exile, and prison. Whatever we have to do, we do it as comrades, in every situation.

APPRENTICESHIP

ADALBERT: A number of farmers were not brisk at killing, but they turned out to be conscientious. In any case, the manner came with imitation. Doing it over and over: repetition smoothed out clumsiness. That is true, I believe, for any kind of handiwork.

PANCRACE: Many people did not know how to kill, but that was not a disadvantage, because there were *interahamwe* to guide them in their first steps. At the beginning the *interahamwe* came in by bus from the neighboring hills to lend a hand. They were more skilled, more impassive. They were clearly more specialized. They gave advice on what paths to take and which blows to use, which techniques. Passing by, they would shout: "Do like me. If you feel you are making a mess of it, call for help!" They used their spare time to initiate those who seemed uneasy with this work of killing.

That instruction happened just in the first days; later we had to shift for ourselves and polish our crude methods.

ALPHONSE: At first you cut timidly, then time helps you grow into it. Some colleagues learned the exact way to strike—on the side of the neck or the back of the head—to hasten the end. But other colleagues were all thumbs right up to the finish. Their moves were slow, they did not dare—they hit the arm instead of the neck, for example, then ran away yelling, "That's it, I killed this one dead!" But everyone knew it wasn't true. A specialist had to intervene, catch up with the target, and dispatch it.

ÉLIE: The club is more crushing, but the machete is more natural. The Rwandan is accustomed to the machete from childhood. Grab a machete—that is what we do every morning. We cut sorghum, we prune banana trees, we hack out vines, we kill chickens. Even women and little girls borrow the machete for small tasks, like chopping firewood. Whatever the job, the same gesture always comes smoothly to our hands. The blade, when you use it to cut branch, animal, or man, it has nothing to say.

In the end, a man is like an animal: you give him a whack on the head or the neck, and down he goes. In the first days someone who had already slaughtered chickens—and especially goats—had an advantage, understandably. Later, everybody grew accustomed to the new activity, and the laggards caught up.

Only young guys, very sturdy and willing, used clubs. The club has no use in agriculture, but it was better suited to their way of trying to stand out, of strutting in the crowd. Same thing for spears and bows: those who still had them could find it entertaining to lend them or show them off.

PIO: There were some who turned out to be easy killers, and they backed up their comrades in tough spots. But each person was allowed to learn in his own way, according to his character. You killed the way you knew, the way you felt it, each at his own speed. There were no serious instructions on know-how, except to keep it up.

And then we must mention a remarkable thing that encouraged us. Many Tutsis showed a dreadful fear of being killed, even before we started to hit them. They would stop their disturbing agitation. They would cower or stand stock still. So this terror helped us to strike them. It is more tempting to kill a trembling and bleating goat than a spirited and frisky one, put it that way.

FULGENCE: The fumblers were followed as a precaution, because of possible incompetence. The *interahamwe* gave them compliments or reprimands. Sometimes, if they wanted to be strict, the penalty was to finish off the wounded person, whatever it took. The culprit had to keep tackling the job to the end. The worst thing was being forced to do this in front of your own colleagues.

We were only a few, at the very start. That didn't last long, thanks to our familiarity with the machete in the fields. It's only natural. If you and me are given a ballpoint pen, you will prove more at ease with writing work than me, no jealousy on my part. For us, the machete was what we knew how to use and sharpen. Also, for the authorities, it was less expensive than guns. Therefore we learned to do the job with the basic instrument we had.

JEAN-BAPTISTE: If you proved too green with the machete, you could find yourself deprived of rewards, to nudge you in the right direction. If you got laughed at one day, you did not take long to shape up. If you went home empty-handed, you might even be scolded by your wife or your children.

In any case, everybody killed in his own way. Someone who couldn't get used to polishing off his victim could just walk on or ask for help. He would find a supportive comrade behind him.

No colleague ever complained of being mistreated for his awkwardness. Mockery and taunts—they could happen, but harsh treatment, never.

LÉOPORD: Me, I took up only the machete: first because I had one at the house, second because I knew how to use it. If you are skilled with a tool, it is handy to use it for everything—clearing brush or killing in the swamps. Time allowed everyone to improve in his fashion. The only strict rule was to show up with a good cutting machete. They were sharpened at least twice a week. This was not a problem, thanks to our own whetstones.

Whoever struck crooked, or only pretended to strike, we encouraged him, we advised him on improvements. He might also be obliged to take another turn at a Tutsi, in a marsh or in front of a house, and to kill the victim before his colleagues, to make sure he had listened well.

JOSEPH-DÉSIRÉ: Bunglers—there were always some of them around, especially at dispatching the wounded. If you are born timid, this is difficult to change, with the marshes running with blood. So those who felt relaxed helped out the ones who felt uncomfortable. This was not serious so long as it kept going.

IGNACE: Some hunted like grazing goats, others like wild beasts. Some hunted slowly because they were afraid, some because they were lazy. Some struck slowly from wickedness, some struck quickly so as to finish up and go home early to do something else. It was not important, it was each to his own technique and personality.

Me, because I was older, I was excused from trudging around the marshes. My duty was to patrol in stealth through the surrounding fields. I chose the ancestral method, with bow and arrows, to skewer a few Tutsis passing through. As an old-timer, I had known such watchful hunting since my childhood.

Jean: "It is a Rwandan custom that little boys imitate their fathers and big brothers, by getting behind them to copy. That is how they learn the agriculture of sowing and harvesting from the earliest age. That is how many began to prowl after the dogs, to sniff out the Tutsis and expose them. That is how a few children began to kill in the surrounding bush. But not in the muck of the swamps. Down there it was too hard for the little ones to move freely. Anyway, it was forbidden by the intimidators."

Clémentine: "I saw papas teaching their boys how to cut. They made them imitate the machete blows. They displayed their skill on dead people, or on living people they had captured during the day. The boys usually tried it out on children, because of their similar size. But most people did not want to involve the children directly in these bloody doings, except for watching, of course."

GROUP SPIRIT

The first thing I felt in front of each member of the group was not aversion, or contempt, or pity, or even antipathy, but distrust: it was immediate and mutual. What I didn't know when our meetings began was that this feeling would never be entirely dispelled, no matter what particular bond I managed to form with each man. With time, the hostility gradually faded. Occasionally I caught myself sharing with them moments of cordiality, or ordinary cheerfulness, chatting about this and that. Yet never for one instant did I feel free of that distrust. Everything about them kept it alive.

Distrust was also in the air during my first meetings with survivors in Nyamata, while I was writing *Dans le nu de la vie*. The wariness was one-sided, however, directed toward me, never the other way round, and their reticence was of a different nature. Besides being suspicious of a foreigner whose compatriots had not lifted a finger to prevent the genocide, the survivors were convinced that it was too late, that there could no longer be any point to their testimony, not when offered to people who had tolerated the massacres. So my whole enterprise was suspect. Even more tellingly, they did not think they would be believed if they recounted what they had lived through during and since the genocide. They also feared their stories might revive their pain. They concluded that they were wasting their time with this intruder, that there was no sense or advantage in speaking up outside the community of those who had escaped the slaughter.

So their distrust was keen, but I found that if I remained mindful of their feelings, time did help to allay their suspicions. Survivors must stay on guard vis-à-vis the outside world, for they now live in their own world of survivors.

The killer, on the other hand, does not dread your disbelief—on the contrary: he fears that you will bring accusations against him. Even if you can convince him that his words will do him no harm, he fears that no matter who his listener is—or later on, his reader—he would be better off remaining silent. And no relationship of trust can completely dispel that anxiety. The killer stays on guard because he feels the threat of punishment hanging over him.

After the publication of *Dans le nu de la vie*, readers asked me how I chose the fourteen Rwandan participants. The answer is simple: I didn't choose them. During a trip to the Bugesera, I met Sylvie Umubyeyi, a social worker, and followed her as she made her rounds. She was searching the bush in the Nyamata area for children who had been abandoned and scattered during the genocide. After telling me her story, she took me to the home of Jeannette Ayinkamiye, a young survivor who had taken refuge with a female friend and some orphaned children in a tumbledown house by a plot of land they were clearing. Then Jeannette told me her story. The charisma of the one woman, the grief of the other, and the gentleness, solitude, and strength they shared introduced me to their world. From their two stories sprang the idea of a book.

The other twelve narratives were those of the first twelve people whom I approached—often by chance—and found willing to try telling their stories. The truth is, they chose themselves. Despite my ingrained reflexes as a journalist, I felt that in the aftermath of a genocide, criteria of age, sex, social class, and cultural background were meaningless; it would have been absurd to put together a representative panel by searching for such-and-such a survivor because he or she had been this or that before the genocide. My fourteen witnesses were mostly women and mostly farmers, simply because they accepted the experiment more spontaneously than did men and intellectuals.

In the course of my subsequent trips to Rwanda, these last reproached me for not allowing them to express—with their intellectual vocabulary and detachment—their different conception of the event. I told them that their initial evasiveness had been understandable as well as significant, but that it would have been stupid and dishonest if I had later replaced one narrative with another, since each was unique.

I got lucky again when—during difficult moments of misunderstanding, renunciation, dejection, or breakdown in the dialogue with certain people—I resisted the temptation to replace some witnesses with others who would be more talkative, more cooperative, or more French-speaking. I kept up the dialogue with each of the original participants, however long it took, until we seemed to get somewhere.

Throughout this work with the survivors, I did not contact the killers. The idea never occurred to me, and the killers meant nothing to me. I never thought of continuing my project with them or of drawing a parallel between the two sets of narratives. That would have been immoral, unacceptable in the eyes of the survivors (in the eyes of readers, too, of course), and uninteresting besides. Out on the hills I occasionally encountered people suspected of being killers, and I'd met many of them in 1994. I could well imagine what they were like. Only at the end of my conversations with the survivors did I feel any wish to visit the prison—out of a sort of ambiguous curiosity sparked by various details and contradictions in the survivors' descriptions.

The idea of actually talking to the killers came much later, thanks to recurrent questions asked by readers of *Dans le nu de la vie*. Their interest was contagious. If people who had been touched or enthralled by the survivors' stories wanted to know what had gone on in the minds of the killers, that meant it was reasonable to try asking them. That said, while I had no doubts about my first project, I was constantly doubtful about this one. I began it skeptically, because the relationship I tried to establish with the killers seemed at first both disheartening and futile—and brutally different from the rapport I had established and have maintained with the survivors and other people in the Nyamata area.

Alone, faced with the reality of genocide, a survivor chooses to speak, to "zigzag with the truth," or to be silent. A survivor who chooses to speak accepts the constant need to question and challenge the confusions of memory.

Faced with the reality of genocide, a killer's first choice is to be silent, and his second is to lie. He may change his mind, but he will not discuss why. Alone, he takes no risks, just as he took none during the massacres. So you cannot plan on questioning him alone, on interviewing a succession of men whom you've chosen independently of one another.

And so I decided—after a string of failures, botched meetings, and insipid discussions—to address not just a series of randomly chosen individuals but a group of prisoners who would feel protected from the dangers of truth by their friendship and joint complicity, a bunch of pals secure in their group identity established before the genocide, when they helped one another out in the fields and downed bottles of *urwagwa* together after work, a group identity strengthened during the chaos of the killings in the marshes and by their present imprisonment.

I selected the ten friends from Kibungo for simple reasons.

Their gang was both ordinary and informal, one of many in the countryside, with no special ties at first, as might be the case with a religious association, a sports club, or an organized militia. They had banded together because of the proximity of their fields, their patronage of a *cabaret*, and their natural affinities and shared concerns.

They lived on the same hills as most of the survivors I had talked to. They had taken part in the carnage in the marshes of Nyamwiza, where the fugitives had gone to hide, burying themselves up to the neck in slime, beneath the vegetation. They were all farmers, except for one civil servant and one teacher; only three belonged to any paramilitary or *interahamwe* organization. Aside from Élie, they had never worn a police or army uniform. None of them had ever quarreled with his Tutsi neighbors over land, crops, damage, or women.

Moreover, Innocent Rwililiza knew them all well, and they knew him. A pupil and then a teacher at the local school, a public scribe in his spare time, the life and soul of several associations, a man of boundless dedication, a beloved and amusing frequenter of numerous *cabarets*, Innocent was well liked in those hills, in particular in Kibungo, where his family farm is located. He was an indispensable intermediary, the ideal collaborator, and a formidable translator whenever necessary.

He has this to say about the gang: "I knew them from way back. I had taught some of them, like Adalbert, Pancrace, Pio. The others I used to run into along the way and share a drink with at the *cabaret*.

"Adalbert was very intelligent and very bold, sly and mean in an ordinary way. Pancrace was tough and hard to read. He's been in Adalbert's shadow since they were little kids. Pio was really quite nice. Alphonse was the wiliest at business but obliging enough with a bottle in front of him. Fulgence thought of himself as a good-looking boy. He was even more dapper than many Tutsis. And very fond of praying.

"Léopord, him, he never got himself noticed for anything but his height. And the fact that what he later did with his machete was dumbfounding. Ignace was a codger and a dodger, plus he'd suddenly go nasty with Tutsis. He always hated them, and said so long, loud, and often to sway his colleagues or make them laugh. But him, he never laughed. He lived on the outs with everyone, even his family.

"In the end, those boys were no different from the others in character. But they went around together. You saw that they shared and shared alike with field work and drink at the *cabaret*. During the genocide I know that gang went out cutting from the first day to the last. At Adalbert's prodding, perhaps, or under the bad influence of Ignace, they became relentless."

TASTE AND DISTASTE

IGNACE: At the beginning we were too fired up to think. Later on we were too used to it. In our condition, it meant nothing to us to think we were busy cutting our neighbors down to the last one. It became a goes-without-saying. They had already stopped being good neighbors of long standing, the ones who handed around the *urwagwa* can at the *cabaret*, since they wouldn't be there anymore. They had become people to throw away, so to speak. They no longer were what they had been, and neither were we. They did not bother us, and the past did not bother us, because nothing bothered us.

ÉLIE: We had to put off our good manners at the edge of the muck until we heard the whistle to quit working. Kindness, too, was forbidden in the marshes. The marshes left no room for exceptions. To forget doubt, we had meanness and ruthlessness in killing, and a job to do and do well, that's all.

Some changed color from hunting. Their limbs were muddy, their clothes were splattered, even their faces were not black in the same way. They became grayish from everything they had done. A little layer of stink covered us, but we didn't care.

PIO: We no longer saw a human being when we turned up a Tutsi in the swamps. I mean a person like us, sharing similar thoughts and feelings. The hunt was savage, the hunters were savage, the prey was savage—savagery took over the mind.

Not only had we become criminals, we had become a ferocious species in a barbarous world. This truth is not believable to someone who has not lived it in his muscles. Our daily life was unnatural and bloody, and that suited us.

For my part, I offer you an explanation: it is as if I had let another individual take on my own living appearance, and the habits of my heart, without a single pang in my soul. This killer was indeed me, as to the offense he committed and the blood he shed, but he is a stranger to me in his ferocity. I admit and recognize my obedience at that time, my victims, my fault, but I fail to recognize the wickedness of the one who raced through the marshes on my legs, carrying my machete. That wickedness seems to belong to another self with a heavy heart. The most serious changes in my body were my invisible parts, such as the soul or the feelings that go with it. Therefore I alone do not recognize myself in that man. But perhaps someone outside this situation, like you, cannot have an inkling of that strangeness of mind.

PANCRACE: Some began the hunts with nerve and finished them with nerve, while others never showed nerve and killed from obligation. For others, in time, nerve replaced fear.

Many displayed nerve while they were working, and fear as soon as the killing stopped. They simply fired themselves up during the melee.

Some avoided the corpses, and others did not give a spit. The sight of those corpses spreading through the marshes, it could put courage into you or weigh on you and slow you down. But most often it hardened you.

Killing is very discouraging if you yourself must decide to do it, even to an animal. But if you must obey the orders of the authorities, if you have been properly prepared, if you feel yourself pushed and pulled, if you see that the killing will be total and without disastrous consequences for yourself, you feel soothed and reassured. You go off to it with no more worry.

JEAN-BAPTISTE: The more we killed, the more greediness urged us on. Greediness—if left unpunished, it never lets you go. You could see it in our eyes bugged out by the killings. It was even dangersome. There were those who came back in bloodstained shirts, brandishing their machetes, shrieking like madmen, saying they wanted to grab everything. We had to calm them with drinks and soothing words. Because they could turn ugly for those around them.

ALPHONSE: Man can get used to killing, if he kills on and on. He can even become a beast without noticing it. Some threatened one another when they had no more Tutsis under the machete. In their faces, you could see the need to kill.

But for others, on the contrary, killing a person drove a share of fear into their hearts. They did not feel it at first, but later it tormented them. They felt frightened or sickened. Some felt cowardly for not killing enough, some felt cowardly for being forced to kill, so some drank overmuch to stop thinking about their cowardice. Later on they got used to the drink and the cowardice.

Me, I was not scared of death. In a way, I forgot I was killing live people. I no longer thought about either life or death. But the blood struck terror into me. It stank and dripped. At night I'd tell myself, After all, I am a man full of blood; all this spurting blood will bring catastrophe, a curse. Death did not alarm me, but that overflow of blood, that—yes, a lot.

Jean: "A boy with enough strength in his arms to hold the machete firmly, if his brother or his father brought him along in the group, he imitated and grew used to killing. Youth no longer hampered him. He became accustomed to blood. Killing became an ordinary activity, since our elders and everyone did it.

"Or a young boy might even prove more at ease with it than an experienced oldster, because death touched him from farther away. Given the novelty of the circumstances and his young age, death seemed less important to him. He saw it as belonging to an older generation. He shrugged off its perils and considered it a distraction."

JOSEPH-DÉSIRÉ: It became a madness that went on all by itself. You raced ahead or you got out of the way to escape being run over, but you followed the crowd.

The one who rushed off machete in hand, he listened to nothing anymore. He forgot everything, first of all his level of intelligence. Doing the same thing every day meant we didn't have to think about what we were doing. We went out and came back without having a single thought. We hunted because it was the order of the day, until the day was over. Our arms ruled our heads; in any case our heads no longer had their say.

FULGENCE: We became more and more cruel, more and more calm, more and more bloody. But we did not see that we were becoming more and more killers. The more we cut, the more cutting became child's play to us. For a few, it turned into a treat, if I may say so. In the evening you might meet a colleague who would call out, "You, my friend, buy me a Primus or I'll cut open your skull, because I have a taste for that now!" But for many, it was simply that a long day had just come to an end.

We stopped thinking about obligations or advantages—we

thought only about continuing what we had started. In any case, it held us so tight, we could not think about its effect on us.

ADALBERT: At the start of the killings, we worked fast and skimmed along because we were eager. In the middle of the killings, we killed casually. Time and triumph encouraged us to loaf around. At first we could feel more patriotic or more deserving when we managed to catch some fugitives. Later on, those kinds of feelings deserted us. We stopped listening to the fine words on the radio and from the authorities. We killed to keep the job going. Some were tired of these blood assignments. Others amused themselves by torturing Tutsis, who had made them sweat day after day.

At the end of the killings, the instructions were to speed things up before the *inkotanyi* arrived. Flight beckoned us, but we had to continue the massacres before leaving. Reinforcements and scoldings put the last touch on the matter; the organizers talked about a final sweep through the marshes. Fear kept telling us to run away, but we were finishing what we had started.

Later, we fled our way through hunger and want on the roads to Congo, but we kept hunting in the ruined houses for forgotten Tutsis. We still had the heart for that.

LÉOPORD: Since I was killing often, I began to feel it did not mean anything to me. It gave me no pleasure, I knew I would not be punished, I was killing without consequences, I adapted without a problem. I left every morning free and easy, in a hurry to get going. I saw that the work and the results were good for me, that's all.

During the killings I no longer considered anything in particular in the Tutsi except that the person had to be done away with. I want to make clear that from the first gentleman I killed to the last, I was not sorry about a single one.

GOING INTO ACTION

Thinking back, with the wisdom of hindsight, to those years that devastated Europe and in the end, Germany itself, we feel torn between two judgments: did we witness the rational development of an inhuman plan, or a manifestation (so far unique, and still poorly explained) of collective madness? A logic bent on evil, or the absence of logic? As often happens in human affairs, both possibilities of this alternative coexisted.

—PRIMO LEVI,
The Drowned and the Saved

At what moment was the decision made? How did the fateful meeting go? Who first spoke of complete extermination? What were the listeners' initial reactions? These questions seem essential. The precise details are more haunting in connection with a genocide than with a civil war, no matter how murderous, barbaric, and cruel such a war may be.

Although we cannot reconstruct the unimaginable scene, we do know that the decision to commit genocide in Rwanda followed the kind of pattern we see in the German implementation of the Holocaust: the Rwandan genocide was the result of plans and preparations formulated essentially by collective decisions.

As soon as they took office, Hitler and the other leaders of National Socialism announced that the Jewish community was unwelcome in Germany. The Nazi party developed more and more initiatives in the government and its departments, a rising tide of acts intended to sweep German society clear of Jews and

Gypsies. Dismissals, confiscations, brutalities, anti-Jewish laws, the wearing of the yellow star; exclusions, deportations, pogroms, confinement within ghettos, in concentration camps . . . Between 1933 and 1940, the regime confirmed with each passing day—with hate-filled speeches, decrees, and murders—that it was determined to exclude the Jewish community from the Third Reich. Still, the Final Solution probably became inevitable for Hitler and his two specialists, Himmler and Heydrich, only sometime in the course of 1941, and the decision to implement it was communicated during the following weeks to his general staff and the officers in charge of the project.

The formal decision to commit genocide was the result of a long process. When was the decision made? when the Jews were declared subhuman, or when they were deported in large numbers to ghettos and concentration camps? at the time of Hitler's famous speech at the Reichstag in January 1939? or, that same year, when a gassing technique was tested on tens of thousands of patients with mental illnesses and incurable diseases, to evaluate its large-scale effectiveness?

Was it after the failure, in September 1940, of the so-called Lublin and Madagascar plans—as outlandish as they were deadly serious—that provided for a complete deportation of Jews to those two destinations? when Himmler, the future master organizer, became second in command in the Nazi regime? during the euphoric initial weeks of the invasion of the Soviet Union in June 1941, when the first *Einsatzgruppen* were sent to the rear of German troops in Russia with orders systematically to shoot all Jews living in the occupied zones?

Or was it three months later, when the SS general staff approved the installation of crematoria in six camps? or on December 12, 1941, the day after the German declaration of war on the United States, when Hitler gathered his chief dignitaries in his home to announce, according to Goebbels's diary, that "world war is here. The destruction of the Jews will be its inevitable consequence"? Even today, many historians research and debate this question, but it remains a mystery.

Although remarkably similar to the Holocaust in the progressive planning that gave it shape, the Rwandan genocide is rooted in its own unique historical reality.

At the time of Rwanda's declaration of independence in 1962, the Hutu leaders who swept into power had emerged from a violent and flawed social movement: the popular revolution of 1959, following on the death of the last Tutsi king. This Hutu uprising overthrew the Tutsi aristocracy and abolished the constraints that the majority Hutu population now deemed unacceptable. The new Hutu leaders championed no ideals worthy of this revolt and cynically used the uprising to marginalize the entire Tutsi community—peasants, civil servants, teachers—from which the aristocracy had sprung. Having conflated the once-privileged Tutsi aristocrat with the hardworking Tutsi peasant, the populist Hutu administration depicted all Tutsis as scheming, treacherous speculators and parasites in an overpopulated country.

A military coup d'état led by Major General Juvénal Habyarimana in 1973 reinforced this policy. To isolate Tutsi citizens accused of underhanded practices, Habyarimana ordered the seizure of goods and property, the uprooting of communities, the imposition of educational quotas, and the passage of exclusionary laws and laws prohibiting mixed marriage (which remained in force until 1976). Above all, he instigated recurrent waves of massacres.

In 1990 rebel Tutsi troops—this was the early Rwandan Patriotic Front—marched out of the Ugandan bush to make war on the Hutu Rwandan army, opening a new phase in the conflict.

All genocides in modern history have occurred in the midst of war—not because they were its cause or consequence but because war suspends the rule of law: it systematizes death, normalizes savagery, fosters fear and delusions, reawakens old demons, and unsettles morality and human values. It undermines the last psychological defenses of the future perpetrators of the genocide. The farmer Alphonse Hitiyaremye summed it up in his own way: "War is a dreadful disorder in which the culprits of genocide can plot incognito."

In 1991, while the attacking Tutsi rebels were gaining ground, speeches at Rwandan political meetings, notably at rallies held by the party of President Habyarimana and his ministers, consisted almost entirely of threats made against Tutsis. In Butare, home of the national university, professors vied with one another to publish historical screeds and anti-Tutsi diatribes. In the broadcast studios of popular radio stations, Radio Rwanda and Radio Mille Collines, the Tutsis were referred to as "cockroaches." Announcers, the two best known of whom were Simon Bikindi and Kantano Habimana, used humorous sketches and songs to call openly for the destruction of the Tutsis.

Innocent Rwililiza remembers: "Those gentlemen were famous artists, great comic virtuosos. What they said was so cleverly put, and repeated so often, that we Tutsis as well, we found them funny to listen to. They were clamoring for the massacre of all the cockroaches, but in amusing ways. For us, the Tutsis, those witty words were hilarious. The songs urging all the Hutus to get together to wipe out the Tutsis—we laughed out loud at the jokes. Same thing for *The Hutu Ten Commandments*, which vowed to do us in. We got so used to these things that we didn't listen to the horrible threats anymore."

Crimes committed against the Tutsis usually went unpunished. Two members of the gang from Kibungo, for example, killed a Tutsi before the genocide without being convicted by the judicial system: Élie Mizinge, the former soldier, admits to the murder of a social worker during a demonstration in 1992; another youth protests his innocence but is implicated in a murder by all the evidence, including testimony from his friends.

Nevertheless, in this propitious climate for killings on a grand scale, the extermination of the Tutsis does not seem to have been considered until the winter of 1993–94, a few months before the downing of Habyarimana's plane set the plan in motion.

ÉLIE: I think the idea of genocide germinated in 1959, when we killed lots of Tutsis without being punished, and we never repressed it after that. The intimidators and the peasants with hoes found themselves in agreement.

As for us, we told ourselves that the Tutsis were in the way, but this idea was not always in our thoughts. We talked about it, we forgot about it, we waited. We heard no protests about our murders. As with farm work, we waited for the right season. The death of our president was the signal for the final chaos. But as with a harvest, the seed was planted before.

The exile of the Habyarimana clan that scattered its important members in the summer of 1994 and the so-called national reconciliation policy of Rwanda's current administration make it difficult today to retrace in detail the path of genocidal directives issued at the highest level.

In the Nyamata district, the burgomaster and subprefect, their most reliable stooges, the big shots of the two main Hutu political parties, a few *interahamwe* leaders, and officers in the army camp at Gako—fewer than twenty people out of a population of 120,000—were informed by Kigali of the precise plan of extermination, probably at the end of December 1993.

UNAMIR* people and the chancelleries of the principal countries involved in the region were also briefed. One month before the onset of the carnage, civil servants at a certain level—school principals, hospital directors, municipal judges—and some businessmen were let in on the secret, for a total of fewer than sixty people.

In Germany, when the decision to commit genocide was actually made, the army, police, government services, and various sectors of civil society—educational institutions, railroads, chambers of commerce, churches—had already long been prepared to carry it out. And the last phase of the destruction of the Jews began without a hitch.

Things in Rwanda went equally smoothly. In the early morning of April 7, six or seven hours after the explosion of the plane, a core group gave the green light; the administration, army, and police went into action. The soldiers were ready, the militias were gung-ho, plenty of machetes were available—many of them brand new—with stout arms to wield them. Spirits were willing. Orders went out across the country. The killings began, one day after another, at different paces in different regions, but nothing hindered the progress of the massacres.

In Germany as in Rwanda, genocide was undertaken by a totalitarian regime that had been in power for some time. The elimination of the Jew, the Gypsy, or the Tutsi had been openly

---

*The United Nations Assistance Mission in Rwanda was dispatched in November 1993 to supervise the implementation of the Arusha peace accords, a cease-fire agreement signed in August of that year between the Rwandan government and the RPF in Arusha, Tanzania. Its initial strength of 2,500 men under the command of the Canadian Major General Roméo Dallaire dropped to 450 men on April 14, 1994, a week after the killings had begun. UNAMIR's intervention consisted of protecting and evacuating expatriates and its own personnel. After French troops initiated and completed this controversial Operation Turquoise in June and July, which was said to be a humanitarian mission but which principally protected the exodus of Hutus to Congo, a new UN mission, UNAMIR II, arrived in August, three months after the end of the genocide.

part of the regime's political agenda from the moment it took power, and had been repeatedly stressed in official speeches. The genocide was planned in successive stages. It thrived in the disbelief of foreign nations. It was tested for short periods on segments of the population.

It was tested in the Bugesera, for example.

ÉLIE: One year was calm, one year was hot. And it would happen again, two calm seasons, one hot. It depended on the attacks by the *inkotanyi*; but it might well depend on us, too. We usually observed certain priorities: teachers and the owners of choice plots of land sat high on the list . . . Afterward we might kill little bunches of Tutsis here and there depending on what situations came up. One year, for example, we pushed hundreds of Tutsis alive into the bog at Urwabaynanga; another year we launched bloody raids in classrooms. We might leave a few bodies beside the road for no good reason except to show off the corpses—and to show what was on our minds. The year 1992 was a burning hot one because of the pressing threat of the *inkotanyi*.

Those killings were not premeditated, they were rough at the edges, but still they went unpunished. They were, in a way, groundwork for the future.

In Germany and in Rwanda, efficient preparations preceded the formal decision on extermination, as if the decision were too appalling to be announced in public until it was already being carried out.

IGNACE: I think the possibility of genocide fell out as it did because it was lying in wait—for time's signal, like the plane crash, to nudge it at the last moment. There was never any need to talk about it among ourselves. The thoughtfulness of the authorities ripened it naturally, and then it was proposed to us. As it was their only proposal and it promised to be final, we seized the opportunity. We knew full well what had to be done, and we set to doing it without flinching, because it seemed like the perfect solution.

FIELD WORK

ALPHONSE: For someone plodding up the slope of old age, that killing period was more backbreaking than stoop labor. Because we had to climb the hills and chase through the slime after the runaways. The legs especially took a beating.

At first the activity was less repetitive than sowing; it cheered us up, so to speak. Afterward it became the same every day. More than anything, we missed going home to eat at noon. At noon we often found ourselves deep in the marshes; that is why the midday meal and our usual afternoon naps were forbidden us by the authorities.

JEAN-BAPTISTE: No one was going to their fields anymore. Why dig in the dirt when we were harvesting without working, eating our fill without growing a thing? The only chore was to bury bananas in pits, out in abandoned banana groves, to allow the next batch of *urwagwa* to ferment. We became lazy. We did not bury the bodies—it was wasted effort—except, of course, if by bad luck a Tutsi was killed in his own field, which would bring a stench, dogs, and voracious animals.

ADALBERT: We roasted thick meat in the morning, and we roasted more meat in the evening. Anybody who once had eaten meat only at weddings, he found himself stuffed with it day after day.

Before, when we came home from the fields, we'd find almost nothing in the cooking pot, only our usual beans or sometimes even just cassava gruel. When we got back from the marshes, in the *cabarets* of Kibungo we snapped up roast chickens, haunches of cow, and drinks to remedy our fatigue. We found women or children everywhere offering them to us for reasonable prices. And brochettes of goat meat, and cigarettes for those who wanted to try them.

We overflowed with life for this new job. We were not afraid of wearing ourselves out running around in the swamps. And if we turned lucky at work, we became happy. We abandoned the crops, the hoes, and the like. We talked no more among ourselves about farming. Worries let go of us.

PANCRACE: Cutting corn or bananas, it's a smooth job, because ears of corn and hands of bananas are all the same—nothing troublesome there. Cutting in the marshes, that was more and more tiring, you know why. It was a similar motion but not a similar situation, it was more hazardous. A hectic job.

In the beginning the Tutsis were many and frightened and not very active—that made our work easier. When we could not catch the most agile of them, we fell back on the puny ones. But at the end only the strong and sly ones were left, and it got too hard. They gathered in little groups, very well hidden. They were picking up all the tricks of the marsh game creatures. When we arrived, too often we would get all mired up for nothing. Even the hunters grew discouraged. Plus, the marshes were rotting with bodies softening in the slime. These were piling up, stinking more and more, and we had to take care not to step in them.

That's why our colleagues grew lazy. They turned their steps in another direction and waited for the signal to go home. They muttered about missing farm work, but they were a small number. Besides, not one of them put in a little hour clearing brush out in the front of his field. Those colleagues were grumbling just because they were impatient to pop a Primus. They were thirsty for more than work. They were getting fed up with the marshes because they felt well off. It wasn't longing for their hoes that made them bellyache, but laziness.

LÉOPORD: Killing was less wearisome than farming. In the marshes, we could lag around for hours looking for someone to slaughter without getting penalized. We could shelter from the sun and chat without feeling idle. The workday didn't last as long as in the fields. We returned at three o'clock to have time for pillaging. We fell asleep every evening safe from care, no longer worried about drought. We forgot our torments as farmers. We gorged on vitamin-rich foods.

Some among us tasted pastries and sweets like candies for the first time in our lives. We got our supplies without paying, in the center of Nyamata, in shops where farmers had never gone before.

FULGENCE: Hunting in the swamps was more unpleasant than digging in the fields. On account of the commotion in the morning, the agitation of the intimidators, and the severity of the *interahamwe*. The changes in habits most of all. Agriculture is our real profession, not killing. On our plots of land, time and the weather know how to organize us with the seasons and sowing; each person cultivates at will what the field will give.

In the marshes, we felt bumped around, we found ourselves too crowded, too carefully penned in. The hubbub in other sectors sometimes bothered us. When the *interahamwe* noticed idlers, that could be serious. They would shout, "We came a long way to give you a hand, and you're slopping around behind the papyrus!" They might yell insults and threats at us in their anger.

We felt far from home. We weren't used to working at the call of a whistle, for going out and back.

But as to fatigue and bounty, it was better. During the growing season, if malaria fevers pin you to your bed, well, your wife or your children go to the fields for food and come home worn out. Or else your empty belly chases away your sleep.

During the killings, passing neighbors dropped off more food than you could fit in your pot—it overflowed at no cost to you. Meat became as common as cassava. Hutus had always felt cheated of cattle because they didn't know how to raise them. They said cows didn't taste good, but it was from scarcity. So, during the massacres they ate beef morning and evening, to their heart's content.

IGNACE: One evening at the rough beginning, we came back late. We had spent the day running after the fugitives. We were tired.

But on the way back, we discovered another group of girls and boys. We pushed them along as prisoners to the judge's house. He ordered that they be sliced up on the spot, in the dark. No one grumbled despite our weariness from an exhausting day. But afterward he assigned us ordinary schedules such as we were used to. That relieved us.

PIO: Farming is simpler, because it is our lifelong occupation. The hunts were more unpredictable. It was even more tiring on days of large-scale operations, patrolling so many kilometers behind the *interahamwe*, through the papyrus and mosquitoes.

But we can't say we missed the fields. We were more at ease in this hunting work, because we had only to bend down to harvest food, sheet metal, and loot. Killing was a demanding but more gratifying activity. The proof: no one ever asked permission to go clear brush on his field, not even for a half-day.

ÉLIE: It was punishment to rummage through the papyrus all day long without coming back to eat at noon. The belly could gripe, and the calves, too, since they were soaking in mud. Still, we ate abundant meat each morning, we drank deep in the evening. That balanced things properly. The looting reinvigorated us more than any harvest could, and we stopped earlier in the day. This schedule in the marshes was more suitable, for the young and especially the old.

IGNACE: Killing could certainly be thirsty work, draining and often disgusting. Still, it was more productive than raising crops, especially for someone with a meager plot of land or barren soil. During the killings anyone with strong arms brought home as much as a merchant of quality. We could no longer count the panels of sheet metal we were piling up. The taxmen ignored us. The women were satisfied with everything we brought in. They stopped complaining.

For the simplest farmers, it was refreshing to leave the hoe in the yard. We got up rich, we went to bed with full bellies, we lived a life of plenty. Pillaging is more worthwhile than harvesting, because it profits everyone equally.

Clémentine: "The men left without knowing what their day's weariness would be. But in any case they knew what they would collect along the way. They returned with tired but laughing faces, tossing out jokes to one another, as in seasons of bumper harvests. It was clear from their manner that they were leading an exciting life.

"For the women, life was restful above all. They abandoned the fields and marketplaces. There was no more need to plant, to shell beans, to walk to market. Simply seeking brought finding. When our columns of Hutu fugitives set out for Congo, they left behind neglected fields where the brush had already eaten up several seasons of farm work."

ALPHONSE: It was a grubby job but a job without worries about drought or spoiled crops, we can certainly say that. On his plot the farmer is never sure what the harvest will bring. One season he'll see his sacks swollen, so his wife can carry them to market, and another season he'll see them flapping thin. He'll think about slinking away from the eyes of the taxmen. He'll show an anxious and sometimes miserable face.

But in the Tutsis' abandoned houses, we knew we'd find quantities of new goods. We started with the sheet metal, and the rest followed.

That time greatly improved our lives since we profited from everything we'd never had before. The daily Primus,★ the cow meat, the bikes, the radios, the sheet metal, the windows, everything. People said it was a lucky season, and that there would not be another.

★ *This Belgian brand is the most popular beer in Rwanda. Brewed in Gisenyi, a city on the western border, across from Goma in Congo, it is sold only in one-liter bottles. Inexpensive, slightly bitter, with a normal alcoholic content, it is drunk lukewarm and straight from the bottle, nursed along in endless tiny sips. Mutzig (brewed in Burundi) and Amstel are two drab rivals of this champion brew.*

A NEIGHBORHOOD GENOCIDE

Rwanda, famous land of a thousand hills, is above all a land of one vast village. Four out of five Rwandan families live in the countryside, and nine out of ten draw more or less all their income from the soil. Every doctor, every teacher or shopkeeper, owns a plot of land on his native hill, which he cultivates in his spare time or entrusts to a relative. Even Kigali, spread over an immense area, seems less like a capital city than a collection of villages linked by little valleys and tracts of open ground.

After the genocide, many foreigners wondered how the huge number of Hutu killers recognized their Tutsi victims in the upheaval of the massacres, since Rwandans of both ethnic groups speak the same language with no distinctive differences, live in the same places, and are not always physically recognizable by distinctive characteristics.

The answer is simple. The killers did not have to pick out their victims: they knew them personally. Everyone knows everything in a village.

At the risk of offending historians of the Holocaust with this quick summary of their work, I would say that most of them—in particular Raul Hilberg, in his monumental study *The Destruction of the European Jews*—see four stages in the unfolding of the event: the first stage brought humiliation and loss of rights; next came designation and marking (armbands, yellow stars, writing on walls); then deportation and concentration; and finally complete elimination, through famine in the ghettos, shooting in the areas conquered by the German army, and gassing in the six specialized camps. These stages overlapped rather than succeeded one another in rigorous succession, and they were linked by continuous repression in the pogroms, as well as by plundering and expropriations, which were important for ensuring the support of a decisive segment of the population. Although German, French, Polish, Rumanian, and Dutch societies, for example, all had different cultures, their urbanization and industrialization gave rise to the same four stages of genocide in each case.

For an urban society, an urban kind of genocide; for a village society, a village genocide. In rural Rwanda, the course of genocide skipped the second and third stages, which were unnecessary, given the close proximity of the killers and their prey.

This observation is oversimplified, however, for in a way the victims *were* singled out: the government had been recording the ethnic background of all its citizens—Hutu, Tutsi, and Twa—on identification papers, employment applications, and other documents since 1931. During the genocide, these papers sometimes helped Rwandan militiamen and soldiers at roadblocks and checkpoints in cities and at the borders, but they were not needed by the immense majority of the killers in the countryside.

The inhabitants of the district of Nyamata all agree that those documents played no part in the killing there. The ethnic background of the region's sixty thousand Tutsis was well known to their neighbors, without exception, even in the case of recently arrived families, civil servants in temporary posts, drifters, and hermits in rickety shacks in the depths of little valleys.

Shortly after the announcement of the attack on President Habyarimana, moreover, the Tutsis gathered *themselves* together, in a spontaneous protective reflex. First, they moved toward hamlets with a concentrated Tutsi population—for example, on the hill of Ntarama; then they took refuge in churches; finally, at the start of the slaughter, they fled into marshes and forests.

Another observation helps to explain the reactions of Rwanda's essentially village society. For twenty years a presidential clan had ruled by requiring absolute allegiance from all leading figures, Hutu and Tutsi alike, and by completely suppressing dissent. This policy drove many intellectuals from Rwanda and undermined the so-called urban petite bourgeoisie, a class that can be the wellspring of careful reflection and protest during periods of grave social instability.

The consequences were dramatic. From the moment the killings began, this petite bourgeoisie—trapped between a clannish dictatorial regime and an omnipresent peasantry, disheartened by the war atmosphere, appalled by the assassinations of respected Hutu and Tutsi figures—could not keep from splitting spectacularly asunder. And the Hutu intelligentsia, far from applying the brakes, rushed for the most part to the front lines of the massacres to affirm its existence in this new era.

As Jean-Baptiste Munyankore, a teacher in Ntarama and a survivor of the marshes, confirms: "The principal and the inspector of schools in my district participated in the killings with nail-studded clubs. Two teachers, colleagues with whom we used to share beers and student evaluations, set their shoulders to the wheel, so to speak. A priest, the burgomaster, the subprefect, a doctor—they all killed with their own hands . . . They wore pressed cotton trousers, they had no trouble sleeping, they traveled around in vehicles or on light motorcycles . . . These well-educated people were calm, and they rolled up their sleeves to get a good grip on their machetes. For someone who has spent his life teaching the humanities, as I have, such criminals are a fearful mystery."

Ignorant of mechanized agriculture and agronomic technology, Rwanda's peasant society made no attempt to modernize the carnage, ignoring all scientific, medical, and anthropological experimentation, employing no efficient industrial techniques such as gas chambers and no ingenious methods to economize effort. The army did not use helicopters, tanks, or bazookas, while lighter weaponry such as grenades and machine guns came only sporadically into play, and then simply for tactical or psychological support.

In the fields, labor was manual. Therefore, the killings in the marshes were manual, and they proceeded at the pace of a seasonal culture.

Alphonse Hitiyaremye says that at one point, "We hurried things up, because the killing season was coming to a close. It promised to spare us the labor of one harvest, but not two. We knew that for the next season, we would have to take up our machetes again for other, more traditional jobs." That remark touches on an absurdly simplistic observation about farming, which figured as an implicit theme throughout my interviews. The members of the gang were not alone in insisting that since Hutus obtained better harvests than Tutsis (whose herds, in addition, had the nasty habit of trampling fields), Hutus should till the soil instead of Tutsis. And it also explains the exceptionally small number of mixed marriages over the decades in a region where people worked, ate, and prayed together.

Innocent Rwililiza puts it this way: "I cannot recall a single case of mixed marriage among the farmers born on the hill of Kibungo. In Rwanda, mixed marriage was, in a way, the privilege of city dwellers and the rich, the privilege of Tutsi merchants or Hutu officers and high-level civil servants—for example, a wealthy Hutu marrying a tall, slender, well-educated Tutsi woman, or a rich Tutsi wedding a Hutu woman to gain advantages from the government. But the farmers saw no advantage and many complications in mixed marriage. Among ourselves, we knew there was no agreement possible, given the division of family fields and the damage from cows. Such land feuds were too dangerous. What mixed couples there were on the hill had arrived from neighboring prefectures already married."

In the land of philosophy that was Germany, genocide was intended to purify being and thought. In the rural land of Rwanda, genocide was meant to purify the earth, to cleanse it of its *cockroach farmers*. The Tutsi genocide was thus both a neighborhood genocide and an agricultural genocide. And in spite of its summary organization and archaic tools, it was outstandingly effective. Its yield proved distinctly superior to that of the Jewish and Gypsy genocide, since about 800,000 Tutsis were killed in twelve weeks. In 1942, at the height of the shootings and deportations, the Nazi regime and its zealous administration, its chemical industry, its army and police, equipped with sophisticated matériel and industrial techniques (heavy machine guns, railway infrastructures, index files, carbon monoxide gas trucks, Zyklon B gas chambers . . .), never attained so murderous a performance level anywhere in Germany or its fifteen occupied countries.

PUNISHMENT

IGNACE: The first day, the district leader sent us teams of youths to verify that every man had heard the orders to assemble. They boarded up the homes of the reluctant ones. They threatened them with fines. They herded them toward Kibungo and gave them big lectures. Those who tried to zigzag found themselves overtaken and set back on the right path. We went straight to the meeting place.

That is how the hunt began. We adjusted to the routine. It was the same thing every day, except that later on there was no need for teams of monitors, since no one hung back anymore.

PANCRACE: It was obligatory. A special group of hothead boys was assigned to search the houses of those who tried to hide. We feared the authorities' anger more than the blood we spilled. But deep down we had no fear of anything.

I'll explain. When you receive a new order, you hesitate but you obey, or else you're taking a risk. When you have been prepared the right way by the radios and the official advice, you obey more easily, even if the order is to kill your neighbors. The mission of a good organizer is to stifle your hesitations when he gives you instructions.

For example, when he shows you that the act will be total and have no grave consequences for anyone left alive, you obey more easily, you don't worry about anything. You forget your misgivings and fears of punishment. You obey freely.

ALPHONSE: At six o'clock in the morning we had to get counted. Someone who had bananas to press could ask for special leave; also someone who was sick; even later on, someone who found he had a broken animal pen could get himself a delay. But the others went. You could dawdle along the way and nap, but you had to go. You did not feel like working? You had to go. Every day without exception you had to join up again.

There is no one on the hill who can say to God, eyes closed in prayer, that he never went hunting.

For someone caught cheating, it could be serious. He had to pay a fine determined by the leader. A big fine for big trickery or repeated trickery—a cash fine, for example two thousand Rwandan francs or even more. A fine just of drink or of sheet metal— that could be negotiated.

FULGENCE: Everybody gathered on the field at Kibungo—the folks from Kanzenze, Kibungo, Ntarama, and on certain days the *interahamwe* who came from Butamwa or farther away. Anyone who sneaked off behind his house was denounced by a neighbor and punished with a fine. Especially at the beginning, when all this was new to us.

Later on you set out jauntily if you took an interest in the killings; you loafed along if you cared only for the looting. If you were sick, you had to explain yourself clearly. If you asked for a day to press some *urwagwa*, you had to furnish your quota of cans. If you were just flagging from too much drink the night before, you could get away with it, everyone understood, but you couldn't do it again soon. Look out, though, if you took advantage to hang around town in broad daylight. There, in front of everyone, if you were caught, you were sent off double-quick.

The hunt was most demanding on the days of huge operations, when we searched behind the *interahamwe* and soldiers. Those fierce young fellows never let go. On those days no one slipped away, because of the severe punishments. Other days were more easygoing, when it was just us hunting.

PIO: We went up every day to the sports ground, then we decided. For the farmers, it was mandatory. Whoever got caught shirking was punished with a fine. Ordinarily it cost two thousand francs, but it depended on the seriousness. If you couldn't pay, you gave a jerry can of *urwagwa* or a piece of good-quality sheet metal. Some were even fined a goat.

An old man who could not work because of weariness paid nothing if he could send a son to hunt in his place. There were even healthy men who sent their wives to replace them for a day on the expeditions, but that didn't happen often because it was not legitimate.

ADALBERT: At the start, the killings were very regulated, but later things were not so strict. Someone who felt tired or wanted to attend to other things, like looting, collecting sheet metal or merchandise, or doing house repairs, he could ask permission and pay a contribution to those jobbing in his place. You showed usefulness in your own way in the killings, or you paid. In any case you weren't forced to kill, as in the first days.

As long as the main activity was progressing properly, as long as you were not protesting out loud, the authorities became more flexible.

The fines varied with the gravity of the fault or the person's purse. It was one thousand or two thousand francs for an ordinary offense, but it could go as high as five thousand if you had overdone it. At first these fines were very punishing for a farmer because of his poverty. Afterward, thanks to looting, they became more acceptable. Especially if the authorities happened to forget about the fines altogether.

Marie-Chantal: "The farmers were not rich enough, like the well-to-do city people, to buy themselves relief from the killing. Some doctors and teachers in Kigali paid their servants or their employees so as not to dirty themselves.

"On the hills, many killed simply to get around their poverty. If they went along on the killings, they did not risk fines, and besides, it could pay off big on the way home. Whoever found a chance to sheet-metal his roof, how could he hesitate?"

IGNACE: If a neighbor noticed you had sneaked off, he might come see you that evening and ask for a small sum, under threat of denouncing you to the judge the next day and making you pay a heavier official fine. If he showed a willing spirit, you profited by reaching agreement with him. That is why, in our group, we arranged among ourselves to cover up our lapses on the sly.

JEAN-BAPTISTE: At first killing was obligatory; afterward we got used to it. We became naturally cruel. We no longer needed encouragement or fines to kill, or even orders or advice. Discipline was relaxed because it wasn't necessary anymore.

I don't know anyone who was struck because he refused to kill. I know of one case of punishment by death, a special case, a woman. Some young people cut her to punish her husband, who had refused to kill. But she was in fact Tutsi. Afterward the husband took part without whining—in fact, he was one of the busiest in the marshes.

If one morning you felt worn out, you would offer to contribute with drink and then you went along the next day. You could also replace killing with other useful tasks, like preparing meals for the visiting *interahamwe*, or rounding up cows scattered in the bush, so they could be eaten. And when your bravery returned, you would take up the tool again and return to the swamps.

FULGENCE: Aside from the fines of money or drink, I know of no case of punishment, like a cudgel or a machete blow, for refusing to obey. Ill treatment might threaten simply if you refused to pay the fine, but that never happened, thanks to the cash from looting.

The rich person hears the news of his fine with more peace of mind—that is certainly something I have learned.

IGNACE: One evening they condemned a Hutu woman to death and cut her in public, to demonstrate a bad example. She had insolently demanded the cows of her Tutsi husband, who had just been slaughtered. Aside from that, no one in Kibungo was cut for punishment. Or even hit.

PANCRACE: People said that some were mistreated for slipping away, but I do not personally know of any such case on our hill. I believe those people were mistreated because of squabbles over looting. There are even wicked colleagues who accused their neighbors, simply to get their hands on a coveted share—a plot of land, for example.

ÉLIE: In the evening, we had to report to the leader about exactly what we had killed. Many boasted, for fear of being taunted or frowned on. That was also a good reason why we did not bury the bodies. Someone suspected of faking could guide the verifiers to the truth.

But you weren't beaten if you behaved weakly during the day. The requirements were not that excessive. You just found yourself poorly rewarded, and that was unfortunate.

LÉOPORD: Mornings I checked the absences. Someone might show up drooping because of too much drink, and that passed because it was a common reason. Also, someone might offer a pressing obligation, like an illness or a piece of business. Anyway, if the reason wasn't valid, the person had to pay a fine or a jerry can of *urwagwa*; it could even go as high as a case of Primus. Some people were beaten, but only if they lied shamelessly.

PIO: Anyone who had the idea of not killing for a day could get out of it, no problem. But anyone with the idea of not killing at all could not let on, or he himself would be killed while others watched.

Voicing disagreement out loud was fatal on the spot. So we don't know if people had that idea.

Of course you could pretend, dawdle, make excuses, pay—but above all you could not object in words. It would be fatal if you refused outright, even hush-hush with your neighbor.

Your position and your fortune could not save you from death if you showed a kindness to a Tutsi before unfamiliar eyes. For us, kind words for Tutsis were more fatal than evil deeds.

SOME THOUGHTS ON
CORRUGATED METAL

The Congolese city of Bukavu, on the edge of Lake Kivu, not far from the Rwandan border, once enjoyed a provincial charm that delighted its inhabitants and all passing visitors. In the summer of 1994, however, the gaiety of its terraces and the sweet singing of its fishermen were swamped by the misery of an immense horde of refugees.

It was late July, four months after the first machete blows, one month after the first mass exodus of Hutus from Rwanda. My most striking memory of my arrival in the city is of sheets of corrugated metal piled up along the unpaved road, in the villages, around the refugee camps, and taller piles in the streets near the market, and even taller ones down toward the river and at the customs station—jubilantly eyeballed, from behind their Ray-Bans, by the big-shot thugs of the Congolese army.

A constant stream of hundreds of thousands of Hutu exiles was fanning out into this area around Lake Kivu. The most exhausted of them lay down on any open ground, while the more vigorous pushed on to camps in the region of the volcanoes, and the most enterprising or richest refugees scattered throughout Bukavu. Some carried a bundle or a child, while others lugged a chair, a basin, or a sack of grain, and the strongest advanced bent double beneath heavy sheets of corrugated metal, which they exchanged for passage across the border, a bag of grain, a ride in the back of a truck, or a place to rest out in a field.

The strangest memory I have of entering Rwanda, right after

crossing the river and heading toward the town of Cyangugu, is again of that endless, surreal procession of corrugated metal porters. Filling smugglers' pirogues to the water line, heaped onto the logs of raft-ferries, in handcarts, beneath the buttocks of passengers in the backs of trucks, carried by one or two people, lying around tents or huts, stacked around camps, on the roads, in the devastated banana groves, and in the depths of the forest, sheets of corrugated metal stretched out between the bivouacs and the refugee columns as far as the eye could see.

Shaken by the genocide just ended, dazed in the throng, a foreigner might naturally have filed away the puzzling sight under the heading of a collective madness, some trauma to be understood later on, and he would have missed the story behind that corrugated metal.

Sheet metal arrived in Rwanda at the same time as the Belgians, immediately after the First World War, and not by accident, since it was intended as roofing for colonial buildings. Tiles covered the colonists' houses, foliage covered the Rwandans' homes, and sheets of metal covered the public buildings where both peoples would be brought together.

The sheet iron of that period was a good centimeter thick, able to last around fifty years, or as it turned out, until independence. With the passage of time and the emancipation of the people, sheet metal became thinner and spread into the towns, their outlying districts, and gradually the hills, to cover almost every dwelling, including the most modest, which have come to be known as *terres-tôles* (sheet metal adobes). The sheet of corrugated metal is now the measure of a habitation. One says, "So-and-so has built himself a house" not "of so many square meters" but "of so many sheets."

The sheets last varying lengths of time depending on whether they have been imported from Europe (the best), Uganda (the most compact), Kenya (the toughest), or manufactured locally, in the Tolirwa factories of Kigando, near Kigali. These homemade sheets are the thinnest (three millimeters), cheapest, and flimsiest. They last around fifteen years, about as long as the adobe walls of the farmers' houses.

After the genocide, humanitarian organizations handed out sheets of compressed papyrus fiber, but their life-span of a few months fooled no one, either as to their usefulness or as to the benevolence of their donors.

Corrugated metal sheets made a tardy but precipitous appearance in the Bugesera in the early 1960s, to roof the houses of the first waves of Tutsi refugees. Light, transportable, and cheap, they are a godsend in a rainy country that does not provide thatch from cereals or savannas. The sheet metal is sold new or used, impermeable or permeable (in other words, with holes). It serves first as an enclosure, until the walls are up, and then as a roof, but its usefulness does not stop there. After the walls have worn out or collapsed, it serves secondhand to build kitchen shelters, toilets, animal pens, and silos in the courtyard. It also enters into the making of doors, shutters, *cabaret* terraces, chests, and coffins for the poor.

Of all the elements of the house (walls, frame, furniture, domestic accessories), the corrugated metal sheet is the only one the villager cannot make with his own hands—hence its commercial value. "Before the war, in Kibungo, people organized lotteries of sheet metal," says Innocent. "Everyone brought in a brand-new sheet, they passed around bottles of *urwagwa*, they drew lots, and the lucky winner left with a new roof. You could also offer them more formally, in a dowry before a wedding, for example."

A nanny goat costs two sheets, an Ankole cow at least twenty.

One sheet clears the slate for about fifteen Primuses. Its price in Rwandan francs depends on its quality and even more on the season. "During a racking drought, the farmer tends to take down his metal roofing to sell and replaces it with strips of plastic. Then prices nosedive," according to Innocent. "Later on, if the harvest proves bountiful, he buys more metal roofing, new or used, and the price looks up again."

Many factors besides drought can feed the secondhand market, including theft. To hear Innocent tell it, "Agile boys can climb onto a roof and, using damp cloths, uncover sleepers during their dreams, then flee into the bush, especially if they know the owners have been partying." Gambling and alcoholism are frequent causes of "uncovering." I shall not mention here the name of a friend in Nyamata who, at the end of a monumental binge, sold his sheets of roofing one after the other for a last little drink for the road and wound up sleeping under the stars.

The most serious impetus for this trade, however, is war, which impoverishes its victims and drives them into exile.

Although metal roofing is the only element of a house that its owner cannot make on the spot, it is also the one he can most easily transport: a few turns of the screw, and it's on the ground next to the bundles. Its standardization makes it usable throughout the Great Lakes region of central Africa. In 1973 the first sheet metal from the Bugesera went into exile with its owners, who in this case were Tutsis fleeing into Burundi. Then Burundian Hutu refugees fleeing the terror of the Tutsi army and the coups d'état at home brought sheet metal with them to their camps in Rwanda. These comings and goings speeded up in the early 1990s with the increasingly intense clashes on both sides of the Burundi-Rwanda border. Still, they gave no hint of what would happen in the spring of 1994.

On May 13 in Nyamata, while the first gunshots from the Rwandan Patriotic Front troops rang out, most of the Hutu killers set aside their machetes, tore down whatever metal was left on their roofs, and packed for the next day's exodus across the country, toward Bukavu or Goma, in Congo. The metal roofing was abandoned or sold along the way or in the camps, or confiscated or extorted during the exodus or at the border, so obviously it did not come home again during the great return of the Hutu refugees in the autumn of 1996. Today, however, on the hills of Kibungo, Kanzenze, and Ntarama, the inhabited houses bear metal roofs once again thanks to international donations, thanks to the repatriated Tutsis who returned in the wake of the victorious Patriotic Front, and thanks, above all, to on-site salvage.

Not all the sheet metal, in fact, went into exile—quite the contrary. Betraying their optimism, many Hutus attached theirs to their roofs before leaving. And some Hutu refugees abandoned theirs in panic a few kilometers down the road, where Tutsi survivors collected it when the killings were over.

Still others, finally, craftily, took the time to hide the sheet metal from their roofs or their pillaging by burying it on the banana farms. In Nyamata people say that the first thing certain prisoners do, after they've been released from the penitentiary in Rilima, is to dig, one moonless night, for their hoards of corrugated zinc, a touch corroded. Occasionally they are too late because, as Innocent explains, "sometimes a farmer chops a hard blow with his hoe into his field, and immediately you see him break into a wide smile. He knows he has just struck a sheet of corrugated metal and come into a tidy sum."

LOOTING

Marie-Chantal: "On the path down below the field, all day you saw a long line of gatherers, backs bent beneath the burden of their fresh looting. They followed along like a thread of ants behind a food scrap."

ÉLIE: In the evening, after the killings, there was time for friendship, and meeting friends brought us light hearts. We would chat about our days, we shared drinks, we ate. We no longer counted up what we had killed but what it would bring us. The killings had made us gossipy and greedy. We now argued only over sharing, especially plots of land and particularly banana groves. Everyone had to keep an eye on the choice banana plantations thick along the banks of the Akanyaru.

ALPHONSE: There were many banquets. On days of large-scale operations, the *interahamwe* and the soldiers from neighboring communes took priority in the looting. They heaped up new radios, fat cows, comfortable chairs, top-quality sheet metal. We locals shared what they left behind. The days of smaller operations were more profitable for us, since we found ourselves again with first pick. When our group went looting together, we got big rewards. The bounty made us forget about bickering. Sometimes we even had to buy the help of a van to carry everything.

Many suddenly grew rich, so rich they didn't stop to count up. Standing by the wayside, they would hail the killers coming back from looting, they'd propose a friendly drink, buy them endless Primus, share meat, and give away radios—to gull these people whom they left empty-handed. The rich were the most familiar with bargaining, since that was their trade from before. They were gathering in sheet metal and suchlike goods for future business.

Us, we felt carefree and contented. We did not haggle. We were not taxed by the commissioners. We drank very well with the money we were sniffing out. We ate the tastiest meat from the cows of those we had killed. We were pleased by the new sheet metal we were bringing home. We slept comfortably, thanks to good nourishment and the fatigue of the day.

IGNACE: The first evening the boss assembled us in Kibungo. He asked the team to form a circle. He demanded that, one by one, we put in the center all the money we had taken from our victims. He said, "No cheating."

When he saw us so discouraged, he thought about it and spoke again in a kind voice. He explained that, the first time, we had to contribute to buy drink and celebrate together, but that afterward we would indeed each save up for himself. This promise gave us satisfaction. We popped some bottles by way of relief.

ADALBERT: Straggling killers let themselves wander away from eager ones so as to lay early hands on loot, but they did not become extra rich. In the evening the eager killers managed very well for themselves and retrieved what they had let escape. They knew they were tough.

At bottom, we didn't care about what we accomplished in the marshes, only about what was important to us for our comfort: the stocks of sheet metal, the rounded-up cows, the piles of windows and other such goods. When we met a neighbor on a new bike or waving around a radio, greed drove us on. We inspected roofs along the way. People could turn mean if they heard about some fertile land already snapped up behind their backs. They could turn meaner than in the marshes, even if they were no longer brandishing their machetes. Me, it so happens, I am strong and vigorous, I had made myself boss. It was a position with advantages for looting.

PANCRACE: After work we would tally up the profit. The money the Tutsis had tried to take with them under their clothes into death. The money of those who had offered it willingly, in hope of not suffering. The money from goods collected on the way home, and the sheet metal or utensils you could sell in the free-for-all, even at laughable prices. We hid rolls of franc notes in our pockets.

For example, if you snagged two bikes, you didn't fuss about cashing one in. You sold it for a losing price, and then you bought drinks calmly.

We were drinking so much the price of drinks was multiplied by three—even by five, once. But the drinker didn't care anymore, thanks to the money from looting.

Some farmers even hid Tutsis they knew for a certain price. After the Tutsis had coughed up all their savings, the farmers abandoned them to the arms of death, without paying them back, of course. Those were crooked deals.

JOSEPH-DÉSIRÉ: The authorities no longer had the ability to plan, to channel. Their orders fell on deaf ears. The massacres had become extraordinary, beyond all reason.

The keenest ones, when they killed, grabbed the possessions of the dead—they wanted everything, right away, not even stopping to finish off their victims. The looting excited them so much, they needed no advice or encouragement. Their greed spread to those who followed, who went crazy in turn.

The poorest ones were excited by the spoils. And the wealthiest, too, because they had enough money to buy loot and stockpile it. Everyone supported these profitable killings.

Clémentine: "The ragged poor who'd had nothing were all at once getting their hands on a sheet metal roof, clothes, kitchen utensils, and sometimes an abandoned field if they scrambled fast enough. Comfort reached out to them.

"There were even tramps who gave up wandering. Suddenly their arms were just as strong as everyone else's. They grew rich before they knew what was happening. They took advantage of their hoarded spoils to pick themselves out a rich wife, someone they would never have dared to mix with before. Thanks to the killings, they now enjoyed great esteem in a woman's eyes."

Valérie: "After the plane crash, *interahamwe* came prowling around the maternity hospital, machetes in hand. The first day of the killings some soldiers arrived. They said, 'If you give us money, we will keep them from coming in.' They demanded exactly two hundred thousand francs. We had hardly any money left, because the white sisters had carried it all off in the armored vehicles of the UNAMIR. But there were many of us—women giving birth, midwives, and mothers who had come seeking refuge because it was the Sainte-Marthe Maternity Hospital. We took up a collection, we got the whole sum together, we paid.

"The next day they came and wanted the same contribution. Some even insisted on Swiss money. We paid, thanks to women who had hidden wads of bills in their clothes.

"The third day we could no longer pay such a sum. The soldiers said it didn't matter anymore, because they could no longer do anything for us. Right after they left, the *interahamwe* came.

There were a lot of them, because they knew this Swiss maternity hospital was richly equipped with sacks of grain, spring mattresses, distilled water, and quality medicines. First they gathered up absolutely everything they found, then they killed everyone they met, sparing no one; finally they searched the bodies of the well-to-do women, to be sure they had overlooked nothing."

LÉOPORD: We began the day by killing, we ended the day by looting. It was the rule to kill going out and to loot coming back. We killed in teams, but we looted every man for himself or in small groups of friends. Except for drinks and cows, which we enjoyed sharing. And the plots of land, of course, they were discussed with the organizers. As district leader, I had gotten a huge fertile plot, which I counted on planting when it was all over.

Those who killed a lot had less time to pillage, but since they were feared, they would catch up because of their power. No one wound up ahead, no one wound up robbed.

Anyone who couldn't loot because he had to be absent, or because he felt tired from all he had done, could send his wife. You would see wives rummaging through houses. They ventured even into the marshes to get the belongings of the unfortunate women who had just been killed. People would steal anything—bowls, pieces of cloth, jugs, religious images, wedding pictures—from anywhere, from the houses, from the schools, from the dead.

They stole blood-soaked clothing that they were not afraid to wash. They stole stashes of money from underwear. Not in the church, though, because of the rotting bodies forgotten after the massacre on the first day.

ALPHONSE: Some killers claimed girls in the marshes; that satisfied them and made them neglect the looting. They figured they'd catch up the next day.

As for savings, our lives were not as carefully calculated as before. Bargaining became less serious, numbers flew happily around. Abundance relieved us of our petty problems. Some old-timers muttered that this looting was spinning our minds in a sinister direction, that the future would set a trap for us. But looking at those wonderful first fruits, who could listen to them?

ADALBERT: In town we would recount the exploits of the day. Some exaggerated their score, hoping to get a more fertile plot eventually or a field in a better location. Spirits heated up fiercely on the subject of land left vacant by those who had been killed. As soon as someone identified by name a farmer cut in the marshes, we palavered over his land that evening. We kept up a possessive attitude.

Even though we were not farming anymore, we still worried about our families' future.

JEAN-BAPTISTE: If the *inkotanyi* had not taken over the country and put us to flight, we would have killed one another after the death of the last Tutsi—that's how hooked we were by the madness of dividing up their land. We could no longer stop ourselves from wielding the machete, it brought us so much profit.

It was clear that after our victory, life would be truly rearranged. The obedient ones would no longer obey the authorities as before, accepting poverty and riches the usual way. They had tasted comfort and overflowing plenty. They were sated with their own willfulness. They felt fat with new strength and insolence. They had cast off obedience and the inconveniences of poverty. Greed had corrupted us.

A SEALED CHAMBER

Africa is the vast stage of eternal migrations that often alter national and regional borders. Rwanda and Burundi are two rare exceptions, living as they have for centuries turned inward. No metropolis, no place of pilgrimage, no natural resources have attracted immigration. Besides, there is little space for newcomers with their own languages and traditions, such as live in all the neighboring countries, for the Rwandan hills—including even the arid Bugesera—are among the most densely populated areas in the world.

Hence the unfortunate absence of other cultures, other ethnic groups, other African communities in Rwanda when events began to unfold.

Two days after the crash of President Habyarimana's plane, massacres were already ravaging some of Rwanda's cities and towns but had not yet begun in Nyamata. A detachment of blue-helmeted UN soldiers in three armored vehicles arrived in the little town, visiting the church, the convent, and the maternity and general hospitals. At each stop they picked up whites—five priests and three nuns in all. Mission accomplished, the convoy turned around and swiftly vanished down the main street.

Valérie Nyirarudodo, a nurse-midwife at the Sainte-Marthe Maternity Hospital, remembers, "They pulled up in front of the gate. They told the three white sisters to pack small bags immediately. They said, 'No point anymore in wasting time with good-byes, right now is good-bye.' The Swiss women asked to bring along their Tutsi colleagues in white caps. The soldiers replied, 'No, they are Rwandan, their place is here. It is better to leave them with their brothers and sisters.' The convoy left, followed by a van of singing *interahamwe*. Of course, soon afterward, the Tutsi sisters were cut just like the others."

Innocent witnessed the passage of the armored cars: "They caused a big panic among the *interahamwe* who were already roving in the streets, heating themselves up with sudden bursts of gunfire. Some of them shouted, 'The whites are here, others will come, they have terrible weapons, it's all over for us!' When they saw the convoy disappear in the dust without even a little stop for curiosity or a drink on the main street, they celebrated with some Primus and shot off the cartridges in their guns as a sign of relief. You could see they felt saved. They were rid of the last stumbling block, so to speak."

At the same time, in Kigali, whites were leaving embassies, offices, monasteries, and universities via road convoys to neighboring countries and an emergency airlift operating out of the Kanombé airport. A very few foreigners sought refuge in guarded villas, but no foreigners were left in Nyamata.

Not one foreigner—priest, service corps volunteer, diplomat, NGO worker—can provide a convincing reason for this immediate and astonishing flight during the opening hours of the killings. In any case, neither danger nor panic can justify such haste. The most telling explanation I have heard so far (food for thought for those who, at every human tragedy, wonder aloud about the usefulness of information and eyewitness testimony) comes from Claudine Kayitesi, a farmer and survivor on the hill of Ntarama, when she says, reversing our proverb: "Whites do not want to see what they cannot believe, and they could not believe a genocide, because that is a killing that overwhelms everyone, them as much as the others." So they left.

Incidentally, Claudine, twenty-one years old at the time, gives this remarkable definition of the event: "I think, by the way, that no one will ever line up the truths of this mysterious tragedy and write them down—not the professors in Kigali and Europe, not the intellectuals and politicians. Every explanation will give way on one side or another, like a wobbly table. A genocide is a poisonous bush that grows not from two or three roots but from a tangle of roots that has moldered underground where no one notices it."

Those three armored cars sent to evacuate the expatriates from Nyamata spirited away the last white eyewitnesses, the priests and nuns who were so influential in this church-going population. A few hours later the first murders began spreading—in a kind of sealed chamber in which the voices of Radio Rwanda and Radio Mille Collines now echoed the more loudly. The announcers had the time of their lives, pepping up speeches, instructions, and comic routines with songs and even taped hymns.

One should pause to consider the leading role of radio during the genocides in both Germany and Rwanda, societies whose cultures were otherwise so different. Neither the Germany of the Third Reich nor the Rwanda of the Second Republic of Habyarimana was in the television era, let alone in the era of the Internet, so radio exerted a decisive influence. But this observation is inconclusive, which is why I will quote from memory—I hope not too inaccurately—a remark made by Serge Daney, a critic and essayist, during the first Gulf War. Contradicting the received wisdom of the time, when media specialists were debating the overwhelming impact on the event of televised images, Daney maintained, "Radio is far and away the most dangerous of the media. It wields a unique and terrifying power, once the state or its institutional apparatus collapses. It casts off everything that might attenuate or sidetrack the force of words. In a chaotic situation, radio can prove to be the most efficient tool of democracy as well as of revolution or fascism, because it penetrates unhindered to the individual's deepest core, anywhere and at any moment, immediately, without the necessary and critical distance inherent in the reading of a text or image."

On the same day that the armored cars came and went, the burgomaster's squad closed the courthouse, threw open the communal jail, and emptied the Catholic and Protestant churches in Nyamata and Ntarama, except for those occupied by refugees. Freed of the accusing eyes of foreigners, the burgomaster and his henchmen thus distanced the Hutus under their administration from places of morality and conscience. The killings spread from the center of town and out to the hills. Three days later massacres took place in both churches: in each one, more than five thousand died in a single day.

ADALBERT: We were well prepared by the authorities. We felt we were among ourselves. Never again did we think even for a moment that we would be hampered or punished. Ever since the plane crash, the radio had hammered at us, "The foreigners are departing. They had material proof of what we are going to do, and they are leaving Kigali. This time around they are showing no interest in the fate of the Tutsis." We witnessed that flight of the armored cars along the road with our own eyes. Our ears no longer heard murmurs of reproach. For the first time ever, we did not feel we were under the frowning supervision of whites. Other encouragements followed that assured us of unchecked freedom to complete the task. So we thought, Good, it's true, the blue helmets did nothing at Nyamata except an about-face to leave us alone. Why would they come back before it's all over? At the signal, off we went.

We were certain of killing everyone without drawing evil looks. Without getting a scolding from a white or a priest. We joked about it instead of pressing our advantage. We felt too at ease with an unfamiliar job that had gotten off to a good start. But time and laziness played an ugly trick on us. Basically, we became too sure of ourselves, and we slowed down. That overconfidence is what did us in.

REJOICING IN THE VILLAGE

ALPHONSE: The first evening, coming home from the massacre in the church, our welcome was very well put together by the organizers. We all met up again back on the soccer field. Guns were shooting into the air, whistles and suchlike musical instruments were sounding.

The children pushed into the center all the cows rounded up during the day. Burgomaster Bernard offered the forty fattest ones to the *interahamwe*, to thank them, and the other cows to the people, to encourage them. We spent the evening slaughtering the cattle, singing, and chatting about the new days on the way. It was the most terrific celebration.

JEAN-BAPTISTE: Evenings the gang would get together in a *cabaret*, in Nyarunazi or Kibungo, it depended. We might also go from one to the other. We ordered cases of Primus, we drank, and we fooled around to rest up from our day.

Some spent sleepless nights emptying bottles and became even wilder. Others went on home to rest after having an ordinary relaxing evening. Rowdies kept on slaughtering cows after the killings because they couldn't put down their machetes. So it wasn't possible to herd the cows for the future, and they had to be eaten on the spot.

Me, I went through those festivities with a pretend smile and a worried ear. I had posted a young watcher to make rounds about my house, but I stayed on the alert. The safety of my Tutsi wife tormented me, especially during the drinking sessions.

FULGENCE: In the *cabaret*, we made comparisons and had contests. Many upped their numbers to increase their shares. Others lowered their numbers because it bothered them to recount the blood spilled and to boast about it. People cheated both ways and made fun of those who exaggerated too obviously. There is one, however, well known today in prison, who bragged of more than thirty victims in one big day, without anyone accusing him of lying.

PANCRACE: The evening atmosphere was festive, but some came spoiling for a fight, their fists clenched or machetes still dirty in their hands, because of badly distributed land. For fields, negotiations got very serious. Since many drank Primus without counting, it could get chancy.

At night the bosses were gone and their authority with them; conditions in town were no longer controlled, as they were in the marshes during the day. It was heated and disreputable. So the women would come looking for their husbands and take them home if they heard they were in bad company.

ADALBERT: Vagabond children, children from the streets of Nyamata, more or less abandoned by misfortune, took part in the marshes. Little good-for-nothings, so to speak. But the educated children of the farmers—they could not go. They contented themselves with the looting activities and the merrymaking on the hills.

ALPHONSE: During the killings, we had not one wedding, not one baptism, not one soccer match, not one religious service like

Easter. We did not find that kind of celebration interesting any-more. We did not care spit for that Sunday silliness. We were dead tired from work, we were getting greedy, we celebrated whenever we felt like it, we drank as much as we wanted. Some turned into drunks.

Anyone who felt sad about someone he had killed really had to hide his words and his regrets, for fear of being seen as an accomplice and being treated roughly. Sometimes drinkers went mean when they had found no one to kill that day; others went mean because they had killed too much. You had to show them a smiling face, or watch out.

Clémentine: "In the evening, families listened to music, folk dances, Rwandan or Burundian music. Thanks to the many stolen audiocassettes, families in every house could enjoy music. They all felt equally richer, without jealousy or backbiting, and they congratulated themselves. The men sang, everyone drank, the women changed dresses three times in an evening. It was noisier than weddings, it was drunken reveling every day."

ÉLIE: We no longer worried about wasting batteries, we turned on all the radios at once. The blast of music never stopped. We listened to dance music and traditional Rwandan songs, we listened to soap operas. We did not listen to the speeches and news anymore.

Basically, we didn't give a hoot what they were scheming up in Kigali. We paid no more attention to events in the country, as long as we knew the killing was continuing everywhere without a snag. Poor people seemed at ease, the rich seemed cheerful, the future promised us good times. We were satisfied with our private celebrations, with eating well, drinking well, and having lots of fun.

Besides, a youth could hide a girl he had brought back from the marshes, to have her behind a pen or a clump of bushes. But when he had had enough or when tongues started wagging, he had to kill her, to avoid a serious penalty.

Clémentine: "I knew the gang well. Those boys were known in Kibungo for bad behavior when they had had a lot to drink. Before the killings, they used to harass Tutsis. They would lay ambushes to throw taunts and punches at them. Some in the gang spoke extreme words against the Tutsis, calling them cockroaches and threatening them with an evil end. The older ones especially did that, and it made the young ones laugh.

"So during the killings, that gang muscled up to the front line in the marshes. They went off together with great strides, they helped one another during the day, they came back staggering beneath loads of spoils. Evenings they spun out all their boasting to demoralize those who hadn't had as good a hunt. They never tired of killing, mocking, drinking, laughing, celebrating. They displayed constant merriment."

LÉOPORD: In the evening, we told about Tutsis who had been obstinate, those who had gotten themselves caught, those who had gotten away. Some of us had contests. Others made predictions or bets to win an extra Primus. The bragging amused us—even if you lost, you put on a smile.

We had sessions with girls who were raped in the bush. Nobody dared protest that. Even those who were edgy about it, because they had received blessings in church for example, told themselves it would change nothing since the girl was marked for death anyway.

Me, I had no taste for such messing around; I didn't like the drink so much, either. I would take a little for solidarity, then go home to bed early, around eight o'clock, to be in shape the next day. Since I was a cell leader, I had to feel always ready.

ADALBERT: There were two kinds of rapists. Some took the girls and used them as wives until the end, even on the flight to Congo; they took advantage of the situation to sleep with prettified Tutsis and in exchange showed them a little bit of consideration. Others caught them just to fool around with, for having sex and drinking; they raped for a little while and then handed them over to be killed right afterward. There were no orders from the authorities. The two kinds were free to do as they pleased.

Of course a great number didn't do that, had no taste for it or respect for such misbehaving. Most said it was not proper, to mix together fooling around and killing.

FULGENCE: In the evening, the atmosphere was very lively. But at night it turned different as soon as I got home. My wife appeared fearful with me. She no longer felt safe, she simply didn't want to do it anymore. She turned away from me. Waking and sleeping separated us—we no longer hoped in the same way. A number of colleagues went looking for sex in the woods just because of a change of climate in their beds.

ÉLIE: We went home full, we had drunk well. That time offered us carefree evenings of enjoyment. It mixed up Good and Evil for us. It showed us a welcoming smile. With my wife, things went normally. She knew that after such a day I could not do without it.

THE DISAPPEARANCE OF
ESCAPE NETWORKS

Once, Sunday was a day for old shoes, kneesocks, jerseys, and a leather ball on the soccer field of Nyamata, for the afternoon belonged to Bugesera Sport. In their purple and white uniforms, this Nyamata team played in Rwanda's second division, attracting thousands of spectators who streamed in every Sunday, men and women who walked through the forests from Kibungo, Kanzenze, and Ntarama, from every hill within thirty kilometers, singing their heads off in the blazing sunshine.

The soccer field lies at the end of the main street, not far from the bustling marketplace and its ring of *cabarets*. Muddy or rocky depending on the season, surrounded by bush dotted with grazing cows and goats, the field is equipped with regulation cast-iron goal posts and is trampled flat by kids competing for playing rights there during the week.

In the team's early days, the barefoot players—"shirtless" against "undershirts"—kicked around a ball of banana leaves right on the main street: this was the pioneering period. Then they dribbled a ball of foam rubber up and down a roughly cleared field, until they got a real rubber ball. That team included both Tutsi and Hutu players—a golden era dating back to the 1970s that saw the arrival of the first cleats and leather balls.

Tite Rushita, jersey number ten, a former star who dominated the game through some fifteen championships, remembers, "There was a rich merchant named François and a prosperous truck-company owner named Léonard. They were rolling in money, so they helped the team out with little advantages. We got brochettes and sweet drinks, and lifts out to the fields. Kids who lived way out could borrow a bike to come in for practice.

"If we pulled off a great win, we could even walk away with a goat or some bags of grain from the happy shopkeepers. Soccer life was profitable. That's how we got strong enough to play two seasons in the first division."

The team's decline began in the early 1990s, which saw an increasing threat from *inkotanyi* attacks and the creation of the *interahamwe* militias. In Nyamata the Tutsi trainer at the time was fired by order of Burgomaster Bernard; the shopkeepers no longer went to the soccer field; the Hutu players, requisitioned for the first political parades and meetings, missed matches and practice sessions.

Tite Rushita is a Tutsi survivor of the marshes. Today he divides his time between training and supervising kids in the afternoon, and Mutzig beers in the evening *chez* Chicago or Marie-Louise. Here is how he sums up the atmosphere among the players in the last few months preceding the genocide: "Before the match, they would show a smile to one another, and out on the field they hid their thoughts, but after the game they no longer shared drinks. The team limped along and got tripped up by piddling opponents."

The star of the last team to play before the killings was Évergiste Habihirwe, Tite's successor—like him a Tutsi, a survivor, and a lefty. He no longer wants to have anything to do with soccer, despite the appeals of friends and local merchants. Wearing a cap jammed tight on his head, he leaves his plot of land only to go to Marie Mukarulinda's *cabaret*, Au Coin des Veuves (The Widows' Place), in Kanzenze. About those times, he has this to say: "Certain days, the Hutu players left practice to attend meetings. When they returned, they would kick us viciously in the ankles. So during the games, rough play won out over finesse. The shooters no longer took good aim at the goals, the songs went silent. Mockery and muttering went rumbling along."

In 1994 Évergiste was raising a herd of Ankole cattle in the meadows above Kanzenze. On the first morning of the massacres, he impulsively sought refuge at the home of Ndayisaba, his closest friend and teammate (a left back), a Hutu who lived a few hundred meters away. "When I arrived in his courtyard, he was holding his machete, and I saw that he had already cut two children. Luckily, time offered me a short breather, and I could get away. At my house it was already too late; I never saw any of them again.

"My runner's legs carried me full tilt through the forest. During the day I kept my head down in the sorghum; by night I scrounged in the dirt for cassava. I would hear my teammates hunting around my house. It was the same guys who used to pass the ball back and forth with me . . . They would yell, 'Évergiste, we sorted through the piles of bodies, we have not yet seen your cockroach face! We are going to sniff you out, we shall work at night if we have to, but we shall get you!' They shouted and quarreled over not catching me. The players were the most dogged in cutting other players. They had that ferocity of the ball in their hearts."

In Marie-Louise's little place, where Innocent's band of friends meets every evening, Tite nods in agreement with Évergiste. "Me, too. The players tried everything to cut me," he says. "They were obliged to. They were famous *interahamwe* thanks to soccer, so they had to shine thanks to soccer. They had to cut well-known players. On the team, not one teammate gave a helping hand to another. Not one closed his eyes in a kind complicity. Anyone who dared try would have been cut to pieces on the spot."

Innocent objects to that last remark: "They were strong and famous thanks to soccer. They had done well thanks to the ball, and they didn't want to stop going down that good path. I don't know if they could have made a deal or two for their former peers, but I do know that not one of them even thought about it.

"However," he adds drily, "there is one known case of a soccer player reaching an understanding—one case of mutual help out of hundreds of players. He was a Tutsi named Mbarushimana, known as Mushimana. He played on the team, he was number six. During the killings, he denounced his Tutsi neighbors, he unearthed hiding places, he tracked on hunting expeditions for the killers. He hoped to save his life by helping them cut his Tutsi teammates. The *interahamwe* used him, and at the bloody end they laid him out across a path, not even pushing him into a ditch."

The team played its last game in February 1994, against Gashora. That Sunday there were five Hutus, five Tutsis, and one son of a mixed marriage—Tutsi mother and Hutu father—by the name of Célestin Mulindwa. Mulindwa is one of the team's three survivors and the only one who still kicks the ball around on weekends, with fellow teachers or the children in his little village.

"We had lived as brother players," he says, "and we parted as enemy brothers. Our love for the ball burst at the first machete blow. You see, nothing survived the genocide. It cut down soccer with a casual swipe, like all the rest."

Two hundred meters from the soccer field, within the parish walls, the Sainte-Marthe Maternity Hospital stands between the church and the general hospital. The establishment employed three nurses, seven more or less accredited midwives, and as many practical nurses, Hutus and Tutsis without distinction. It provided seven beds for sick babies, four for premature infants, two beds in private rooms, and the convalescence ward.

From the first hours of the killings, while a huge crowd sought refuge in the church, a few hundred women with their children (most of whom had recently been born there) headed for the maternity hospital, which became a women's bivouac. And on the second day the white nuns went off in the UN's armored cars.

"They left us their advice and their supplies of porridge. But since we had never seen them prepare it, we did not know how to eat it," explains Valérie Nyirarudodo, one of the Rwandan nurses. "The female personnel remained, along with the new mothers and their babies, and the women with young children who had come for shelter. There were also two men—our handyman and a cleaning woman's husband who had fixed up a hiding place under the floorboards. There was also a cow in the pen, which the handyman milked to nourish the toddlers."

Valérie is a Hutu, born on the hill of Kanazi. Today she lives in a pretty cottage on a tree-lined street in Nyamata, where she feels more comfortable raising her children. She is shy, quite dignified, speaks impeccable French, and still devotes all her energy to her work at the maternity hospital.

"When the Swiss nuns left," continues Valérie, "they gave me the key and told me not to open the door to anyone while they were gone. Nevertheless, from that day, soldiers came to take money from us, and they came back every morning. One morning a woman arrived to give birth, it was the first happy event of the killing time, but since she was accompanied by threatening *interahamwe*, we did not let her inside. Day and night young men with machetes cruised closer and closer.

"One day a nurse arrived in a jeep of *interahamwe* to point out cheaters. She knew that we had distributed all our smocks in the cupboard to girls because we had heard the killers would not hurt maternity personnel. We could see the problem was growing serious in Nyamata and on the hills, but we never thought it would come to a maternity hospital. I was even bringing my own children to work, for more security.

"The day of the appalling slaughter in the church, a soldier came to get his mother-in-law at the hospital. He told me quietly, 'We won't be coming back. It's over. Get out, run away, those who can.' At the door some *interahamwe* shouted, 'Those who are not targeted, leave. Afterward we won't be able to do a thing for you. The same fate will find you all!' We heard screams outside, we saw the dirty machetes, we knew they had finished the job at the church. All signs indicated that the fatal moment was almost upon us.

"A young man from Kanazi arrived all out of breath and came over to me. 'I came from Kanazi to fetch you,' he said. 'It's your brother who sent me rushing here. Luck is waiting for you, outside, for you and your children. She is impatient for you know what—don't make her wait . . .' I looked at the mama who had just given birth in front of me on a mattress, lying there with her two children. I prayed at top speed, My God, tell me the one I should take. Then I thought, If I take the newborn, I can't feed it since I have no milk. The older one will be easier. I put him in a cloth sling on my back and told the soldiers, 'He is mine, too.' "

Outside in the garden, Valérie watched what followed: "They surrounded the maternity hospital. They ripped down the gates, they simply shot up the locks. They wore very handsome cartridge belts of highly polished leather, but they wanted to avoid wasting bullets. They killed the women with machetes and clubs. Whenever one of the more agile girls managed to escape in the commotion and get out a window, she was caught in the gardens. When a mama had hidden a child underneath her, they picked her up first, then cut the child, then cut its mother last. They didn't bother to cut the nursing infants properly. They slammed them against the walls to save time, or hurled them alive on the heaps of corpses."

Her faltering voice has almost faded away. "That morning, we were more than three hundred women and children. That evening in the garden, there were only five women left, spared because they were lucky to be born Hutu. And one child: his name is Honnête, and he was taken to Kenya to live with his aunt."

People who have lived through a war often tell wonderful stories about friendships, incredible romances, amazing gestures of solidarity, comical and poignant collaborations between protagonists in enemy camps, or humble and admirable deeds. It all provides material for novels, songs, films, and evenings of memories, and it patches things up between you and humanity. French and German conscripts chatted across the trenches and swapped tins of potted meat; Algerian *fellaghas* hid French colonists with whom they played cards; a Vichy minister foiled the deportation of a colleague with whom he went to school. It was the same in Vietnam, Ireland, Lebanon, Angola, El Salvador, Israel, Chechnya—in the name of passion, childhood, a clan, elemental things like affection or loyalty.

During the height of the ethnic cleansing operations in Bosnia-Herzegovina, during the worst of the sieges of Sarajevo and Gorazde and the massacres in Foča and Brčko, lovers met secretly, coffee and sheep were smuggled, there were hideouts and escapes and secret reunions, as well as conversations across the front lines to exchange news about children or mistresses. At Vukovar, besieged and flattened by artillery, a slender path through cornfields provided a safety valve that was common knowledge among the Serbian tank crews. And at the end of the war we were dumbfounded to learn about the thousand and one touching anecdotes we could never even have imagined.

In Nyamata, however, we find not one comradely impulse among teammates, not one gesture of compassion for helpless babies at the breast. No bond of friendship or love that survived from a church choir or an agricultural cooperative. No civil disobedience in a village, no rebellious adolescent in a gang of budding toughs. And not a single escape network, although it would have been easy to set one up in the forty kilometers of uninhabited forests between the marshes and the Burundi border; no convoy, no links among the herders' paths, no web of hiding places to allow the evacuation of survivors. Is this a particular characteristic of genocide? Yes, essentially, despite the too-rare exceptions here and there. This special characteristic should be emphasized, as the word *genocide* is becoming more and more compromised, bandied about by political figures, journalists, and diplomats whenever they speak of particularly cruel killings or carnage on a massive scale.

All wars generate savage temptations that are more or less murderous. The bloodthirsty madness of combatants, the craving for vengeance, the distress, fear, paranoia, and feelings of abandonment, the euphoria of victories and anguish of defeats, and above all a sense of damnation after crimes have been committed—these things provoke genocidal behavior and actions. In other words, panic or explosive fury and the desire to crush the enemy once and for all lead to massacres of civilians and prisoners, campaigns of rape and torture, deadly deportations, pure devastation in all directions. Sometimes nonmilitary actions result as well: the poisoning of rice fields with pesticides, the slaughter of buffalo herds, the forced conversions to foreign religions and cultures. But to confuse these war crimes—even when they tend, in their collective insanity, to destroy a civilian community—with an explicit and organized plan of extermination is a political and intellectual mistake, symptomatic of our culture of sensationalism.

Is this distinction rhetorical claptrap? Is it even possible to distinguish a genocide amid the chaos of war? The answer to both questions lies in another question, a simple and decisive one: who are the victims of choice?

In war, men are killed first, because they are the most apt to fight back; the next targets are women liable to help them, and boys because they try to continue the conflict, and then older men who can offer wise counsel. But in a genocide, the killers track down everyone, in particular babies, girls, and women, because they represent the future.

Here is one example, taken from Srebrenica (with which I am most familiar), but it could be from Katyn, Grozny, My Lai, Basra, or Shatila. On July 11, 1995, the Bosnian Serb army and militias entered the besieged city. Part of the population tried to flee through the forests, while others sought refuge in the UN camp at Potocari. In three days around eight thousand men, most of them civilians, were captured in the surrounding area, dumped by the truckload onto paths and plowed fields, and mowed down with Kalashnikovs or machine guns. Hundreds of them were sadistically humiliated and tortured before their deaths. Women were stopped along the roads and raped; others were killed or mutilated by the explosions of mines or grenades while crossing open fields with their children.

During the same period, almost all the other women, girls, and children—around sixteen thousand people—were safely conveyed to Tuzla, in Bosnian territory. The massacre in Srebrenica was the result of extraordinary planning. The idea of genocide did cross the minds of Serb nationalists in Pale and Belgrade, but if they had decided to implement that idea, they would have systematically machine-gunned the women and children, who perpetuate the life of their communities, in Foča in April 1992 and then in Srebrenica in July 1995.

That said, what purpose does it serve to distinguish one massacre from another when they reach such a scale? Is it not imprudent to pronounce categorically upon episodes of ongoing history? Is not the pain of the victims immeasurable? Is not the savagery of Srebrenica or Grozny as cruel as that of Nyamata? For those who experienced it, it is. For the rest of us, the barbarity of Nyamata is more harrowing because it was absolute.

"War happens when authorities want to overthrow other authorities to take their own turn at the trough. A genocide— that's when an ethnic group wants to bury another ethnic group. Genocide goes beyond war, because the intention lasts forever, even if it is not crowned with success. It is a final intention," says Christine Nyiransabimana, a farmer, in an astonishing echo of the "final solution."

WOMEN

PANCRACE: I think that women are guided by their husbands. When a husband goes out in the morning to kill and comes home in the evening with food, if the wife lights the fire under the cooking pot, then it is because she supports him in the traditional way. My wife did not lecture me, she did not turn away from me in bed. She reproached me only on those days when I overdid it.

FULGENCE: The women showered us sometimes with advice, sometimes with reproaches. Some women showed pity for their Tutsi neighbors and tried to hide them for a few days. But if they were caught, the women did not risk anything except getting their husbands in trouble. My wife scolded me several times—she warned me I might well lose my head in the marshes. I told her that these killings could no longer be stopped. She asked me above all to keep my mouth shut.

PIO: In the Rwandan family, the man is the first one responsible for right and wrong actions, in the eyes of the authorities and neighbors. If a woman wanted to hide Tutsi acquaintances, she had to get permission from her husband, because if she was found out, of course he was the one condemned by his neighbors to cut those acquaintances with his own hand, in public, right in front of his house. It was a punishment of some importance. It was a big thing to cut a person with whom you had shared years both good and bad.

The women were less deciding, they were less punishable, they were less active. They were in the second rank in that activity of genocide.

But really, in the Tutsi camp it was quite the opposite. The killings were more serious for the wives than for the husbands, if in addition they were raped at the end and saw their little ones get cut before their eyes.

JEAN-BAPTISTE: It is a country custom that women do not concern themselves with any bothersome task of cutting. The machete is for a man's work. This was as true for the farming as for the killing.

So during the killings, the women continued to prepare the meals in the morning, and during the rest of the day they went looting. They were storing up goods instead of crops, so they were not unhappy. They didn't complain because they knew that in any case the operation was intended to succeed completely. They dared not show any sign of disagreement with the men's brutality, not even the simple gesture of a mama's kindness.

In Ntarama I do not know of a single Hutu woman who hid away a little Tutsi child to save it from the massacre of its family. Not even a toddler wrapped in a cloth or a nursling unrecognizable to her neighbors because of its tender age. Not one woman on the whole hill cheated in the way of a rescue, not even for a short moment of trying.

ADALBERT: The women led a more ordinary life. They housecleaned, they tended to the cooking, they looted the surrounding area, they gossiped and haggled in town. There were fierce wives who wanted to march off on expeditions and help with the killing, but they were prevented by the organizers, who lectured them that a woman's place was not in the marshes. I know one case of a woman who bloodied her hands out there, a too quick-tempered woman who wanted a reputation for herself.

Still, if women happened to come upon some Tutsis hidden in an abandoned house, that was different.

Marie-Chantal: "When my husband came home in the evenings, I knew the disturbing gossip, I knew he was a boss, but I asked him nothing. He left the blades outside. He no longer showed the slightest temper anymore in the house, he spoke of the Good Lord. He was cheerful with the children, he brought back little presents and words of encouragement, and that pleased me.

"I don't know of any wife who whispered against her husband during the massacres. Jealous wives, mocking wives, dangerous wives—even if they did not kill directly, they fanned the burning zeal of their husbands. They weighed the loot, they compared the spoils. Desire fired them up in those circumstances.

"There were also men who proved more charitable toward the Tutsis than their wives, even with their machetes in hand. A person's wickedness depends on the heart, not the sex."

JEAN-BAPTISTE: During the killings, much jealousy spilled from the mouths of our women because of the constant talk about the Tutsi women's slender figures, their smooth skin thanks to drinking milk, and so on. When those envious women came upon a Tutsi searching for food in the forest, they called their neighbors to taunt her for crawling around that way all slovenly. Sometimes women shoved a neighbor to the bottom of the hill and threw her bodily into the waters of the Nyabarongo.

ALPHONSE: My wife would tell me, "Listen, really, going every day, every day, it's too much. These filthy things should be stopped," and suchlike recommendations I ignored.

One evening she scolded me, "Alphonse, be careful. Everything you are doing will have accursed consequences, because it is not normal and passes all humanity. So much blood provokes a fate beyond our lives. We are going toward damnation." Around the end she refused to share the bed, she slept on the ground, she said, "You are cutting so many, you cannot count them anymore. I am afraid of this foul thing. You are turning into an animal, and I won't sleep with an animal."

IGNACE: I did not hear many women protesting against Tutsis being raped. They knew this work of killing fiercely heated up the men in the marshes. They agreed on this, except of course if the men did their dirty sex work near the houses.

Any wife who wished to tag along on the hunting raids got sent back by her husband, who asked her to mind the house and see to the looting.

ÉLIE: It was impossible for the women to squabble with their men over those killings and the foolish sex matters. After all, they themselves had to go looting, too, to deal with hunger, since the crops were being neglected. The men, the women—no upset came between them during the killings. The men went out to kill, the women went out to pillage; the women sold, the men drank; it was the same as with farming.

LÉOPORD: The women vied with one another in ferocity toward the Tutsi women and children that they might flush out in an abandoned house. But their most remarkable enterprise was fighting over the fabrics and the trousers. After the expeditions they scavenged and stripped the dead. If a victim was still panting, they dealt a mortal blow with some hand tool or turned their backs and abandoned the dying to their last sighs—as they pleased.

PANCRACE: In a war, you kill someone who fights you or promises you harm. In killings of this kind, you kill the Tutsi woman you used to listen to the radio with, or the kind lady who put medicinal plants on your wounds, or your sister who was married to a Tutsi. Or even, for some unlucky devils, your own Tutsi wife and your children, by general demand. You slaughter the woman same as the man. That is the difference, which changes everything.

FULGENCE: The Hutu women imprisoned at Rilima are more fragile than the men, because they are never visited and fed by their husbands or their brothers. Many of them were denounced by envious people, to get the possessions of their dead husbands. They know themselves to be rejected by the past and the present. Which is why they are more reluctant to admit their crimes. When they have done what they have done, they keep silent.

Christine: "Today I worry about that, because many Hutu women have soaked their hands in the blood of genocide. Men are more liable to kill and to reconcile than women. Men forget more quickly, they share the killings and the drinks more easily. Women do not yield in the same way, they keep more memories.

"But I also know of good women, Hutus, who do not dare show compassion for fear of being accused in their turn."

Clémentine: "The men came home from the marshes with savage faces. They behaved brusquely and glowered at the least little household problem. The women viewed their brutality with fear. A few viewed them with anger and muttered against their bloody deeds, especially those like me who had been married to Tutsis they had killed. But most of them said they were content with everything brought back from the killings—like the sacks of beans, the clothing, the money. They went themselves to collect sheet metal and household utensils overlooked by looting husbands.

"Neighbor women asked me how I could have let myself be impregnated by a cockroach. They'd warn me not to hope for anything for my husband, since their men were firmly resolved to kill everyone. They advised me to teach my son that he hadn't had a Tutsi father, that he was a full-blooded Hutu, because if he ever let his tongue slip later on, it would be deadly for him.

"In Nyamata the midwives returned to their jobs at the maternity hospital after the slaughter as though they had not seen any bloody marks upon the walls. They even snagged their last pay before leaving for Congo.

"On the hill of Kibungo not a single woman took in the child of a Tutsi neighbor who had gone to his death. Not one woman mixed a nursling in with her own brood. Not even for money. Not even in a forest hideout. Because the women did not want to be scolded by their husbands, if the men came home punished by a fine for that misdeed."

IN SEARCH OF THE JUST

t was close to noon on April 11, the first day of the Tutsi hunt on the hill of Ntarama. Isidore Mahandago was sitting on a chair in front of his *terres-tôle* house, resting after a morning of weeding. He was a Hutu farmer, sixty-five years old, who had arrived twenty years before in Rugunga, on the Ntarama hill.

Some strapping fellows armed with machetes came singing up the path that ran near his house. Isidore called to them in his deep old voice and lectured them in public, in front of the neighbors: "You, young men, are evildoers. Turn on your heels and go. Your blades point the way toward a dreadful misfortune for us all. Do not stir up disputes too dangerous for us farmers. Stop tormenting our neighbors and go back to your fields." Two killers approached him, laughing, and without a word cut him down with their machetes. Among the band was Isidore's son, who according to witnesses neither protested nor stopped to bend over the body. The young men went on their way singing.

Isidore Mahandago is the Just Man of Ntarama.

The next day, three kilometers away in the bush of Kibungo, Marcel Sengali was watching a herd of brindle Ankole with their lyre-shaped horns. The Sengali family lived in Kingabo, an area inhabited by Tutsis and by three Hutu families, including the Sengalis, who over time had learned from their neighbors how to raise cattle. Because of their mutual trust and friendship, the residents had combined their animals in a single herd.

Coming up the path, Hutu toughs armed with machetes spotted Marcel Sengali on the slope below among the cows, in the shade of a huge *umunzenze* tree. They sprang to the attack and, without even questioning him, hacked him to death. Searching the dead man's jacket, they discovered the word *Hutu* on his identity card and their bloody mistake.

Two days later Marcel's widow, Martienne Niyiragashoki, decided to follow her Tutsi neighbors, her lifelong friends, into the marshes where they were trying to escape the hordes of killers. Her son, Gahutu, was one of them. Learning of his mother's flight into the papyrus swamps, he went down to the edge of the bog several times to order her to come out, screaming promises of his protection. She refused each time, unlike other Hutus who, having first sought refuge in the marshes, usually in the company of a spouse, eventually abandoned their relatives and the swamp to save their own lives. Martienne's body was found much later, cut to pieces.

Marcel Sengali and Martienne Niyiragashoki are the Just of Kibungo.

François Kalinganiré was an influential civil servant in Kanzenze. He had even been burgomaster of Nyamata in the 1980s but was deposed in 1991 because he joined a moderate political organization when Rwanda's multiparty system was created. His tenure as director of the youth vocational center in Mayange had been without incident, although his adversaries still held a grudge against him.

On April 12, the second day of the slaughter, some of them appeared at his home, accompanied by *interahamwe*. Knowing he was married to a Tutsi, they ordered him to kill her to show support for the genocide. He refused stoically and forbade them to enter his house. Terrified by the confrontation, his neighbors urged him to obey by sacrificing his wife. Instead, he tried to get rid of his visitors. He was murdered in his courtyard and buried on his property.

He is the Just Man of Kanzenze.

Joining these people, born in the region and known to us by name, are the anonymous Just. In the forest of Kayumba, looming above Nyamata, around five thousand souls struggled to escape the bloodbath, among them Innocent, Benoît the cattle breeder in his felt hat, Théoneste the ladies' tailor, and other friends who were wary of the churches and the marshes. Unlike those who remained motionless in the slime beneath the papyrus fronds, the fugitives of Kayumba sprinted and slalomed all day long among the eucalyptus, to evade the hunters hot on their heels and survive until nightfall.

One night Innocent encountered three strangers leaning against some trees, resting as they awaited the dawn. "They were Hutus who were not from here," remembers Innocent. "From Ruhengeri, I think. We call them *abapagasi*, guys who come to be day laborers on large plantations in exchange for food. We questioned them politely. They had not gone astray; they said that they were Pentecostalists, and Holy Scripture forbade them to kill men whom the Good Lord had created in His image. And since the authorities forbade them to leave the area, they had gone into the forest.

"In the chaos of the running chases, we lost track of them. Afterward I tried to discover their fate, but I never even heard any talk of them. Were they cut down in the melee? Did they manage to escape to their native region? Nobody knows. In any case, we were twenty survivors in the forest at the end, and they were not among us."

Those three agricultural workers are the unknown Just who surely represent other anonymous good souls.

. . .

And the Just who are still alive, who and where are they? In truth, after many visits and much searching, I have not yet met any of them on the three hills of Kibungo, Ntarama, and Kanzenze. But I can mention some other worthy people in their stead. Ibrahim Nsengiyumua, a prosperous merchant of Kibungo, paid fine after fine to avoid killing and looting, to the point of ruining himself. He did it "because he had amassed enough wealth in his life not to spoil it with blood," explains Innocent.

Valérie Nyirarudodo brought her little ones to her job at the maternity hospital one morning and left with an extra toddler. A mama, living in a house at the foot of the forest of Kayumba, slapped her children because they denounced Tutsis hidden in the bush. Many people, in the words of the young farmer Christine Nyiransabimana, "were able to pretend, to dawdle behind and return in the evening without dirtying their machetes . . . but had to show they were with the others."

In closing, one should mention the special case of spouses in mixed marriages who saved their wives and a few relatives in spite of the merciless sanctions. Unlike the Nazi administration, which generally classified Jewish spouses in a mixed marriage according to their religious faith and instruction, Jewish or Christian, and decided their fate on that criterion, the Habyarimana regime applied a more simplistic, sexist rule. Tutsi husbands of Hutu wives had to be executed, and they were, without exception. Tutsi wives of Hutu husbands could be spared, and sometimes their children with them—that is, if their husbands accepted conditions that Jean-Baptiste Murangira sums up as follows: "Tutsi wives of poor Hutus had to be killed, but their children could be spared. Tutsi wives of well-off Hutus could be saved if the husbands participated conspicuously in the killing duties."

Thus the census taker Jean-Baptiste Murangira saved his wife

Spéciose Mukandahunga; the judge Jean-Baptiste Ntarwandya saved his wife Drocelle Umupfasoni; the retired chief warrant officer Marc Nsabimana saved his wife Annonciata Mukaligo; the director of the post office and a few other prominent citizens and prosperous farmers protected their wives. Following his spontaneous confessions about "the killing duties," the census taker was sentenced to a prison term. Thanks to testimony in his favor, the judge was released after two years in prison; his case is closed, but he has not been reappointed to the bench. Subpoenaed as a witness in several trials and repeatedly summoned to appear before a tribunal, the retired warrant officer has not been prosecuted to this day. Whether they admit or deny their guilt, all three have little to say about their behavior during the genocide and seek no public recognition for their actions.

ACQUAINTANCES

ADALBERT: It was possible not to kill a neighbor or someone who appealed for pity, gratitude, or recognition, but it was not possible to save that person. You could agree together on a dodge, decide on a trick of that sort. But it was of no use to the dead person. For example, a man finding someone with whom he had popped many a Primus in friendship might turn aside, but someone else would come along behind and take care of it. In any case, in our group, that never happened.

FULGENCE: You could spare a person you owed an old favor to, or who had given you a cow, but there was always someone bringing up the rear who was out to kill. Luck did not exempt a single Tutsi in the marshes. What had to be done was done under all circumstances. You knew it, and in the end you did not dare go against that truth.

PIO: Advancing as a team, we would run into a scramble of fugitives hiding in the papyrus and the muck, so it was not easy to recognize neighbors. If by misfortune I caught sight of an acquaintance, like a soccer comrade, for example, a pang pinched my heart, and I left him to a nearby colleague. But I had to do this quietly, I could not reveal my good heart.

Anyone who hesitated to kill because of feelings of sadness absolutely had to watch his mouth, to say nothing about the reason for his reticence, for fear of being accused of complicity. In any case, those feelings did not last long—they managed to be forgotten.

ALPHONSE: We killed everything we tracked down in the papyrus. We had no reason to choose, to expect or fear anyone in particular. We were cutters of acquaintances, cutters of neighbors, just plain cutters.

Today some name acquaintances they supposedly spared, because they know these are no longer living to contradict them. They tell the tales to attract the favor of suffering families, they invent rescues to ease their return. We joke about those fake stratagems.

ÉLIE: We were forbidden to choose among men and women, babies and oldsters—everyone had to be slaughtered by the end. Time was hurrying us on, the job pulled us along, and the intimidators kept saying, "Anyone who lowers his machete because of somebody he knows, he is spoiling the willingness of his colleagues."

Anyway, someone who avoided the fatal gesture before a good acquaintance did it out of kindness to himself, not to his acquaintance, because he knew it brought no mercy to the other person, who'd be struck down anyhow. Quite the contrary, the victim might wind up cut more cruelly, for having slowed up the job for a moment.

FULGENCE: It was possible not to bloody your arms when faced with an acquaintance, but it didn't save the victim's life. The acquaintance would be cut anyway by the next one along. If you avoided a neighbor, that person might be cut more slowly, and you could be fined if you were seen avoiding the victim. Nobody won in the end. It soon became useless to try to spare a neighbor's life. Just one time I saw someone spared: a tall girl taken away by a colleague for shared convenience; not long afterward, a few days at most, she was condemned and thrown into a ditch.

PANCRACE: Since the Tutsis were scattered in the depths of the bush and the marshes, it was hard to leave in the morning with an idea of whom you would find. You took what the papyrus offered.

Still, some people tried to kill one person in particular. You could tell this obsessed them, to be first at the finding. They searched as if they were sniffing around, then got steamed up when they failed. Maybe because of some old falling out, maybe just for fun. Maybe most often so as to get, that very evening, a well-placed field coveted for a long time. Someone who brought proof of an important cutting—a well-known person, or somebody very fast, for example—might be rewarded by a first claim on the victim's land. But usually we hunted without such thoughts.

IGNACE: Anyway, the authorities never gave us any orders to look for some acquaintance as a priority. In the papyrus, we had to strike all we found, because we didn't know in advance what we'd find. No one was to monopolize anyone else's time to get personal victims for himself. At every opportunity, you killed.

LÉOPORD: Our Tutsi neighbors, we knew they were guilty of no misdoing, but we thought all Tutsis at fault for our constant troubles. We no longer looked at them one by one; we no longer stopped to recognize them as they had been, not even as colleagues. They had become a threat greater than all we had experienced together, more important than our way of seeing things in the community. That's how we reasoned and how we killed at the time.

ALPHONSE: The leader would repeat, "Kill everyone except the Tutsi women properly possessed by Hutu husbands, if these show exemplary behavior in the killings." Which explains why some Tutsi women—for example Jean-Baptiste's wife—were spared with the knowledge of their neighbors. But on the contrary, a Tutsi husband of a Hutu woman had to be killed as a top priority, with his wife and their children too, if she made any protest.

ÉLIE: A Tutsi wife, you could try to save her. You offered a cow to the leader and a radio or the like to the organizers, then you handed out small payments of money to those who were prowling around your house. But that wasn't even worth trying if you did not want to cooperate.

A Tutsi husband you couldn't bargain for; he was at the head of the list. If his wife began to argue, she was struck right away, and they cut her husband while she watched, to discourage her. If she kept on, she'd be cut herself with her children.

ADALBERT: Someone who wanted to save his Tutsi wife was required to show great enthusiasm in the killings. Someone who behaved weakly or timidly knew it was all over for his wife. Grousing or idleness doomed her.

JEAN-BAPTISTE: I know the case of a Hutu boy who fled into the marshes with the Tutsis. After two or three weeks they pointed out to him that he was Hutu and so could be saved. He left the marshes and was not attacked. He had spent so much time with Tutsis in his early childhood that he was a bit mixed up. His mind no longer knew how to draw the proper line between the ethnic groups. Afterward he did not get involved in the killings. That is the sole exception. The only able-bodied person not forced to raise the machete, even coming along behind. It was clear his mind was overwhelmed, and he was not penalized.

FULGENCE: It was much better to kill strangers than acquaintances, because acquaintances had time to stab you with an intense look before receiving the blows. A look from a stranger pierced your mind or memory less easily.

Marie-Chantal: "For a woman, it was unthinkable to hide an acquaintance, even if you had been close to her since childhood, even if she gave you small sums of money. When the news got around of a concealed survivor, you had to give her up without delay to your neighbors. You might even be forced to kill her with your own hands. So it did not save her, besides lasting a few days longer for nothing, and it obliged you to do the most sickening work of the men."

Innocent: "I had quite a dear friend to whom I had given a cow. He was a very well-off merchant, obliging, most cordial in every circumstance. Formerly he had asked me to give extensive supplementary instruction to his son to help him pass the national examination. I would come, I would teach, I felt quite at ease at his house, as if in my own home. He and his wife would invite my wife and me to share meals, drinks, and little gifts.

"The day of the killings, I naturally thought of him. I sent to ask him to hide my child. He did not come to his door. He sent word through his houseboy that no one should step inside his courtyard, that there was no longer room in his home for the slightest memory of a friendship.

"Recently, I saw him again several times in prison here, while I was with you. We exchanged traditional embraces of greeting. He behaved kindly, as before. He told me, 'Innocent, you are a little brother to me. You saved your life, and I rejoice in that. But if the situation returned, I would do the same. With such a fate, there is no choice.' "

Francine: "There are killers who whispered the names of acquaintances as they lifted up the papyrus, promising them protection. But it was a simple ruse to encourage them to rise from their watery hiding place, to cut them without the trouble of a search. It was very dangerous to be discovered by an acquaintance, because he could make you suffer for the show of it."

Berthe: "Before, I knew that a man could kill another man, because it happens all the time. Now I know that even the person with whom you've shared food, or with whom you've slept, even he can kill you with no trouble. The closest neighbor can turn out to be the most horrible. An evil person can kill you with his teeth: that is what I have learned since the genocide, and my eyes no longer gaze the same on the face of the world."

PENITENTIARY WALLS

When we read accounts of war experiences or live though periods of war, we are amazed at how bravely people confront their fear and resist the temptation to flee while they still can. Such resistance is fed by courage, hope, and illusion, by blindness and naïveté, and by fatalism as well.

During the Second World War, for example, the refusal of many Jewish communities to recognize the growing threat of extermination and to react before the ghettos and borders were sealed off is astonishing even today. More recently, in Bosnia-Herzegovina, the Muslims' blindness to the destructive raids and ethnic cleansing going on all around them—even when neighboring villages went up in flames—and their stubborn insistence on staying put until the inevitable arrival of the militias' trucks are as incomprehensible as they are admirable. And so it is in Lebanon, in Sierra Leone, and in Chechnya, where people surrounded by ruins cling to their homes and put off any possible escape into exile.

This is why, at the end of the Rwandan genocide, when two million Hutus so suddenly rose as one within a few days in the early summer of 1994 to begin their exodus, we understood that they were fleeing from more than the weapons and vengeance of the RPF troops. Without thinking it through clearly, we sensed that a psychological force much greater than the simple survival instinct was at work to impel that immense throng so powerfully toward Congo—abandoning houses, properties, professions, habits, all without hesitation or a backward glance.

Two years later those families returned from the refugee camps to their plots of land still bearing their collective guilt. Their sense of shame is haunted today by the dread of suspicion, punishment, and revenge, and it mingles with the Tutsis' traumatic anguish and infects the atmosphere, aptly described by Sylvie Umubyeyi: "There are those who fear the very hills where they should be working their lands. There are those who fear encountering Hutus on the road. There are Hutus who saved Tutsis but who no longer dare go home to their villages, for fear that no one will believe them. There are people who fear visitors, or the night. There are innocent faces that frighten others and fear they are frightening others, as if they were criminals. There is the fear of threats, the panic of memories."

After a genocide, the anguish and dread have an agonizing persistence. The silence on the Rwandan hills is indescribable and cannot be compared with the usual mutism in the aftermath of war. Perhaps Cambodia offers a recent parallel. Tutsi survivors manage to surmount this silence only among themselves. But within the community of killers, innocent or guilty, each person plays the role of either a mute or an amnesiac.

In Nyamata I maintain cordial and sometimes even friendly relations with Hutu families. I have conversations with women who are above reproach—with people who have been cleared of all suspicion. I talk with relatives of killers behind their houses, out of sight; I have chatted under the cloak of anonymity in Africa and Europe with exiled former functionaries of the Habyarimana regime. None of those conversations are of particular interest, and some of them are absurd. Bad faith, lying, and denial compete with unease and fear as soon as the subject of the genocide is raised.

It was not difficult to obtain sincere and detailed accounts from soldiers in Vietnam, from torturers for the Argentine dictatorship or in the Algerian war, from militiamen of the ethnic cleansing in Bosnia-Herzegovina, from secret policemen in the Iraqi or Iranian detention camps—sometimes by following the maxim of Oscar Wilde, "Give a man a mask, and he will tell you the truth." But in the wake of a genocide, the evasion of the ordinary killers and their families passes understanding, and it cannot be explained simply by fear of reprisal.

When I went to the regional penitentiary at Rilima, I hoped to attach faces and voices to the killers whom the survivors had mentioned in their accounts. One characteristic of these narratives was that, hidden in the mud beneath the papyrus, the survivors almost never saw the killers, and could describe them only through their movements and shouts during the hunts.

I went to the prison with the expectation that conversations there would be as awkward and useless as they were with Hutu families out on the hills. My intuition was mistaken: from the first, the discussions with the detainees were of a different nature, much more direct and concrete. Subsequent visits confirmed my hunch that only an *imprisoned* killer, a killer who has not yet lived at liberty, can or will tell his story. Clearly, the freer the Hutus were on their land, the less free they were with their words. Conversely, the thicker the prison walls, the more these narratives were encouraged; the walls protected their authors from victims who might recognize a name and condemn them, from colleagues and neighbors who might accuse them of betrayal, and from children who would feel ashamed of them.

Witness the fact that when Ignace—the first of the gang to be released from the penitentiary, because of his age—returned to his home in Nganwa in January 2003, after our interviews, he grumbled about his participation in the book and refused to talk about things he had discussed and that we had recorded in the garden at the Rilima prison.

Very quickly, however, it turned out that those prison walls were no guarantee that a killer would speak. Dialogue with a killer must also occur at a particular moment in his life as a prisoner: after the judicial inquiry into his case has been closed and he has been condemned to a more or less long sentence—in other words, when he knows his account can no longer affect the judicial decision and he believes he will not be confronting the outside world for quite a while.

He must also have taken the momentous steps of admitting, however guardedly, to more or less voluntary participation in the massacres, and of agreeing to describe some of his criminal actions. No matter what scheming and trickery he may be up to, that the killer acknowledges involvement is in fact indispensable. If he denies everything or automatically shifts his responsibility onto others, if he rejects the slightest individual initiative, if he disowns intellectual support for the project and denies any interest or pleasure in carrying it out, we are right back with the litanies recited by all the families on the hills: "It wasn't me, it was the others." "I wasn't there, I didn't see anything." "If the Tutsis hadn't run away, it wouldn't have happened." "I didn't want to, but they made me do it." "If I hadn't done it, someone else would have done it worse." "I had nothing to do with it, the proof is, I have always had Tutsi friends . . ."

Thus the importance of speaking to a group, in this instance a group of pals from Kibungo who were together from the beginning, who accepted and discussed among themselves the conditions of the interviews, who consulted with one another between meetings, and who confronted together their memories as killers.

SUFFERING

ADALBERT: There were some who brutalized a lot because they killed overmuch. Their killings were delicious to them. They needed intoxication, like someone who calls louder and louder for a bottle.

Animal death no longer gave them satisfaction, they felt frustrated when they simply struck down a Tutsi. They wanted seething excitement. They felt cheated when a Tutsi died without a word. Which is why they no longer struck at the mortal parts, wishing to savor the blows and relish the screams.

FULGENCE: The suffering brought to light each person's natural kindness or wickedness. There were fierce people who urged us to cause pain. But they were the very few. Most appeared uneasy with the awful suffering.

We always finished our jobs properly. Except with runaways who had made us sweat too much running in the swamps, of course. I did notice that those carrying guns never aimed at fugitives when they wanted to scatter them; they shot into the air to avoid sending them toward too swift a death.

PANCRACE: Torture was a supplementary activity, resulting from an individual decision or a small meeting. It was just a distraction, like a recreational break in a long work day. The orders were simply to kill.

Some killed slowly because they were afraid, others because they were weaklings, others because it was all the same to them, others from ferocity. Me, I struck quickly without worrying about it. I did not think about such fiendishness, I was hurrying to get through the day's schedule.

ALPHONSE: Some amused themselves with their machetes on the Tutsis, to show off their skill to everyone. They would swagger around boasting later in the evening. Some slowed down their machetes just for punishment. If a Tutsi had worn out a pursuer in a running chase, he could be teased with the point of a machete—it could be nasty for him. It was like demonstrating the bad example, except no one was left alive to notice.

JEAN-BAPTISTE: Extreme agonies were worked on important people, well-known businessmen. It was to punish them for past misdeeds or make them cough up their hidden savings. Also torments were done to people with whom there had been a stubborn grievance—a bargain that had not been settled or bad blood over some trampling by cows, for example. But not often. No orders were given about this. The bosses would say, "Kill, and fast, that's all. There's no point in taking your time."

In Congo, on the way back, I knew some perpetrators who were driven by madness into Lake Kivu. Fright plunged them into an engulfing grave. They thought death would welcome them more mercifully in the waters than on the hills. Horrible threats were flying in all directions as the return drew close. Terror gave them detailed promises of a wretched death, since they had themselves cut a great many in a vicious way. But they were the exceptions.

PIO: There was voluntary suffering and involuntary suffering, so to speak. Because numerous Tutsis ended screaming from cuttings simply because of poor technique. They were the wounded left writhing, through haste, carelessness, or disgust with what had just been done more than through cruelty. Those were sufferings through sloppiness.

LÉOPORD: I saw colleagues linger over their catch to make the agony last. But often they left before polishing someone off because they were too eager to go looting. For example, they gave the first machete blow and then spotted a bike, and—hop, they'd rather jump on the bike than finish the job. Same for a roof with good sheets of corrugated metal. It was greed more than wickedness. I trusted that there was time for each of those occupations. I struck fast and true, I struck just to get it done.

ÉLIE: Making someone suffer was up to each person, as long as he did his job. The intimidators gave no particular order to encourage or discourage it. They repeated, "Just kill, that is the main thing." We didn't care. If a colleague had to play around with a victim, we kept going. But I have to say that the coups de grâce were not well done. Even if it was not from meanness, it was not done nicely.

ALPHONSE: Saving the babies, that was not practical. They were whacked against walls and trees or they were cut right away. But they were killed more quickly, because of their small size and because their suffering was of no use. They say that at the church in Nyamata they burned children with gasoline. Maybe it's true, but that was just a few in the first-day turmoil. Afterward that did not last. In any case I noticed nothing more. The babies could not understand the why of the suffering, it was not worth lingering over them.

FULGENCE: When we saw Tutsis wriggling like snakes in the marshes, it made the guys laugh. Some let them crawl awhile longer for more fun. But that was not the case for everybody. Some didn't care one way or the other and didn't bother with that mockery. If it was easier to catch them crawling, that was better, and that was all.

ADALBERT: When we spotted a small group of runaways trying to escape by creeping through the mud, we called them snakes. Before the killings, we usually called them cockroaches. But during, it was more suitable to call them snakes, because of their attitude, or zeros, or dogs, because in our country we don't like dogs; in any case, they were less-than-nothings.

For some of us, those taunts were just minor diversions. The important thing was not to let them get away. For others, the insults were invigorating, made the job easier. The perpetrators felt more comfortable insulting and hitting crawlers in rags rather than properly upright people. Because they seemed less like us in that position.

Clémentine: "Sometimes the men returned from an expedition pushing a fugitive in front of them. They would stop him in the marketplace. They would take off his watch and shoes. Occasionally they would take off his clothes as well—at least at the beginning of the killings, because afterward the runaways were so tattered, there was nothing left worth taking off.

"These doomed victims were usually acquaintances who had tried to cheat—to pass for Hutu, for example. Or people who had been rich and important before. Or acquaintances disliked because of old quarrels.

"The killers would call everyone to watch. All the women and children would gather to see the show. There were people still carrying drinks, or nurslings on their backs. The killers would cut off the victims' limbs, they would crush their bones with a club, but without killing them. They wanted them to last. They wanted the audience to learn from these torments. Shouts would rise up from all sides. These were raucous village jamborees, quite rare and quite popular."

Jean: "During the killings there was no more school, no more leisure activities, no more ballgames and the like. When there was a cutting session in public, in the church or in the center of town, all the children came running. You weren't obliged one way or the other. Anyone who had not heard about it was attracted by the cries. We studied all the details of the blood. You could squeeze up close or hang back, depending on your curiosity. Those were our only group pursuits."

Sylvie: "All the little children saw public killings. Even if they refuse to talk about it today, they sometimes let slip words that prove they saw those torture shows. They had to watch them, for the lesson and the diversion. The oldest, over twelve or thirteen, could even participate sometimes. Even if they did not kill with their own hands, they went off with the dogs to nose out the fugitives in their bush hideouts. That was what they did during all those weeks with no school, no games, no church. Along with looting.

"It is impossible to give a number, but many children killed. Some say they were sickened by it, scared of it, but were forced to cut by their mamas or papas. Most are completely silent when they hear talk of the killings, even from years ago. Keeping silent blocks both judgment and change."

LÉOPORD: One day an official declared, "A woman on her back has no ethnic group." After those words, men would capture girls and take them to their fields for sex. Many others feared their wives' reproaches and raped the girls right in the middle of the killing in the marshes, without even hiding from their comrades behind the papyrus.

There are girls who saved their lives that way, sometimes for a long while that is still going on. Especially if they were caught by soldiers, who had no one at home. Falling into the hands of farmers, obviously that couldn't last.

Clémentine: "My Tutsi husband had fled into the marshes. The first week of the killings, I had given birth in an abandoned house because they had set our home on fire. Passersby would squawk about the newborn. They jabbered at the door: 'She's one of ours all right, but her son is Tutsi. He has lost his place among the living.' When the men became too threatening, I had to lie down beneath them to save the little one's life. Since they spoke of it among themselves, it happened often."

PANCRACE: Often in the talk of evenings and even in the old days, people would say, "Look at those Tutsis, how they seem so tall. That's why they show themselves so proud and consider us inferior people. That's why their daughters are so prized." So when the killings came, if a killer with a jaundiced eye caught a tall girl in the reeds, he might well strike her in the legs, at the ankles for example, and the arms likewise, and leave her cut shorter without the fatal blow. Even if she was not that tall, as long as she was a woman.

GUYS IN GOOD SHAPE

Two paths lead to the penitentiary in Rilima. One is a sandy track linking the villages of Nyamata, lying prostrate in the heat. The other is a footpath that cuts across the savanna; it allows families from the three hills to walk to the prison in seven to ten hours, depending on the weight of the bundles they bring on visiting days.

The beige-brick penitentiary rises like a fortress on a hill overlooking Lake Kidogo and, in the distance, the marshes of the Nyabarongo River, which reappears in the landscape after a detour. Everywhere else lie vast desert wastes of arid soil and brush, dotted here and there by green oases of stoic corn and beans. Rilima reigns over the driest part of the Bugesera.

In *Dans le nu de la vie*, I wrote: "The outside wall of the prison, without barbed wire or watchtowers, sits atop a small hill. An orange iron gate lets authorized prisoners slip in and out. From fifty meters away, one is struck both by the orchestral din of competing rhythms and songs and by a suffocating stench of sweat, backed up by the reek of cooking and garbage. One look through the opening in the gate gives an idea of the indescribable promiscuity of life within those walls."

Two years later, nothing had changed. The population was still around seven thousand five hundred prisoners in premises built to house a third of that number. The detainees slept five hundred to a block in metal bunk beds, usually on mattresses of blankets and cardboard. About five hundred slept in the prison yard, sheltering under plastic tarps.

Despite this overpopulation, however, prison conditions have improved so much—thanks to international funding, the politics of national reconciliation, and the daily intervention of the Red Cross—that they are now superior to the public hygiene of the villages on the surrounding desert plateaus, especially during droughts and malaria epidemics. The Rwandan government supplies cornmeal and cassava flour, beans, firewood, and two hours of electricity each day. The Red Cross furnishes the rest: oil, cleaning supplies, bedding, medicines, and impeccably cut prison uniforms of a striking pink.

Reveille is at five-thirty. Those who begin the day with prayer awaken one another a half-hour earlier. At six it's time for water duty: a constant back-and-forth of men fetching cans of water on their backs from the lake, some forty thousand liters for drinking and washing. The sole meal of the day is served, block by block, from nine in the morning until three in the afternoon, supplemented by extras obtained from the prisoners' families and on the black market.

During this time, work squads go off to the penitentiary's 173 acres, to local construction sites, and to workshops for clock and watch making, mechanics, metalwork, and hairdressing. The labor, which is optional and unpaid, provides only modest advantages, except at the prison kitchens, which fatten up the lucky kitchen staff as well as the legal advisers, supervisors, and preachers who draw their salaries directly from the cooking pots. The clergy of many churches share the afternoons for religious services and divide up Sunday in two-hour slices.

All inmates are allowed to receive visitors twice a week. But after the hours of walking and of waiting outside the prison walls, the families may speak with the prisoners for a few moments at most, and the hubbub—of exclamations, commands, and hastily delivered food—is quite depressing. Most prisoners have had only one or two visits since their incarceration began. This lack of connection with the outside world increases their isolation.

The guys in the Kibungo gang are in good physical and psychological shape, adequately fed and cared for. They must put up with the crowding and lack of privacy, but they suffer no hardship or deprivation that might affect their behavior toward us.

Following Innocent's advice, I contact first the two people with the most influence in the group: Jean-Baptiste Murangira, the former civil servant from Ntarama who today heads an association of repentant killers, and Adalbert Munzigura, yesterday the *interahamwe* boss in Kibungo, today a prison security captain and still leader of the gang. After these two give their approval, we meet with the others to explain the project and discuss the rules with them.

For our part, we promise to divulge nothing in our interviews to any judges, lawyers, or prison officials, to any of the gang's drinking buddies in Nyamata, to any relatives of victims, or to any of the gang's own families, and to publish our findings only after their trials, definitive verdicts, and sentencing, so that their accounts may neither help nor hinder them.

Their collective collaboration is rewarded with supplies of sugar, salt, soap, sodas, and medicines from a list they draw up. Another highly valued token of our appreciation is the news we bring them of their families, whom we visit briefly in the afternoons to pass on their messages.

For their part, the men are free to withdraw from the project at any time, temporarily or permanently, without repercussions on their colleagues. As it turns out, none will choose to leave.

They must all follow the same procedure when they don't

want to answer certain questions: if they find a question unpleasant or embarrassing, they are to remain silent or briefly state their unwillingness to reply, explaining their refusal if at all possible. But they must promise not to lie or to say just anything.

That last rule, seemingly so simple and approved at the outset, quickly becomes the subject of exhausting, sometimes tense discussion, because the men cannot help using, for Innocent and me, the defense mechanism they created to protect themselves from the judicial system, their families, or their own consciences: mixing lies, more or less spontaneous or tactical, into their accounts. This forces me to break off the interviews with two of the gang and exclude them from the group, because their insistence on elaborating impossible stories, refusing to face facts, and hiding behind foolish nihilism gets us nowhere.

After an initial period of misunderstandings and uncertainty, however, the others gradually adapt to "zigzagging with the truth" only through silence, and in the end they "zigzag" less and less. Each one zigzags in his own way, though; some of them go off in a great curve that seems to go on forever, while others merely take a short sharp turn on occasion, as we shall see.

For example, Pio or Alphonse, who tend to follow the gang's lead, observe the rules faithfully once they are on their own. Léopord refuses outright to play the trump card of silence and answers all my questions. Adalbert is unpredictable; one day he says anything at all, another time he speaks with perfect frankness. Sometimes Élie feels the need to pour out his heart, and sometimes he doesn't. Ignace and Jean-Baptiste always play things close to the vest . . .

In spite of our rules, the accounts presented here certainly contain a few lies, one or two that I know of and others I may not have discovered yet. For example, the circumstances surrounding Jean-Baptiste's first murder do not jibe with his description. A Hutu farm woman who witnessed it says that Jean-Baptiste was not singled out and forced to kill his first victim as he claims, but was on the contrary quite willing, so much so that he went on to cut down an elderly couple near the *cabaret* he mentions. After some hesitation, I chose to leave Jean-Baptiste's version alone, because despite its deliberate falseness, it does reflect a more essential truth about the frenzy of the mob mentality and the blackmail used against the husbands of Tutsi wives. And there are exceptions to every rule.

The Rwandan government was cooperative: the minister of the interior granted us permission to visit the prison and conduct interviews there without restrictions.

The warden of the penitentiary set three conditions: First, the meetings had to take place outside the inner enclosure housing the sleeping blocks and the prison yard, to avoid drawing crowds of onlookers. Second, because of his death sentence, the interviews with Joseph-Désiré Bitero had to be conducted under the surveillance of an armed guard sitting ten meters away. This had no effect on the interviews because at that distance the guard—who couldn't have cared less—could not hear our conversation, and anyway he didn't understand French, which Joseph-Désiré Bitero, a former teacher, spoke fluently. Third, the interviews were to be suspended on Sunday, the day of rest.

AND GOD IN ALL THIS?

ADALBERT: The Saturday after the plane crash was the usual choir rehearsal day at the church in Kibungo. We sang hymns in good feeling with our Tutsi compatriots, our voices still blending in chorus. On Sunday morning we returned at the appointed hour for mass; they did not arrive. They had already fled into the bush in fear of reprisals, driving their goats and cows before them. That disappointed us greatly, especially on a Sunday. Anger hustled us outside the church door. We left the Lord and our prayers inside to rush home. We changed from our Sunday best into our workaday clothes, we grabbed clubs and machetes, we went straight off to killing.

In the marshes, I was appointed killing boss because I gave orders intensely. Same thing in the Congolese camps. In prison I was appointed charismatic leader because I sang intensely. I enjoyed the alleluias. I gladly felt rocked by those joyous verses. I was steadfast in my love of God.

One day, singing hymns at the top of my lungs, I felt uneasy at taking pleasure in their religious words without ever speaking of what I had done to the killed. I looked around at all my praying colleagues in prison uniforms. I thought, We pardon those who have offended us on earth as in heaven, and we muddle over everything we did in the marshes. I thought, Our songs fly up so loud, they must certainly be heard outside the prison. All those blessings promised in the Book to people of good faith tormented me because of my bad faith.

That's why I agreed to begin confessing a little, first to God, then to the authorities, and why I agreed to tell you.

ALPHONSE: The Thursday when we went to the church in Ntarama, the people just lay there in the dim light, the wounded visible between the pews, the unhurt hiding beneath the pews, and the dead in the aisles all the way to the foot of the altar. We were the only ones making a commotion.

Them, they were waiting for death in the calm of the church. For us, it was no longer important that we found ourselves in a house of God. We yelled, we gave orders, we insulted, we sneered. We verified person by person, inspecting the faces, so as to finish off everyone conscientiously. If we had any doubt about a death agony, we dragged the body outside to examine it in the light of heaven.

Me, I had been sincerely baptized Catholic, but I felt it preferable not to pray traditionally during the killings. There was nothing to be asked of God during that filthy business. Still, to get to sleep some nights, I could not help bowing down in secret to ease some gloomy fears with a timid "Sorry."

PANCRACE: Men are not created by God in the same way. There are killers with good hearts who agree to make confession. There are killers with hard hearts who feed their hatred in silence. They are very dangerous because faith does not soften their character. They never miss a scheduled religious session. They throw themselves wholeheartedly into prayers and hymns, they observe all the religious gestures like signs of the cross, kneeling, and the like. They seem gifted for religion, but deep down they know they must begin to kill again. They are waiting patiently for the next opportunity.

FULGENCE: I was a deacon, the one who made arrangements for Christian gatherings on the hill of Kibungo. In the priest's absence, it was I who conducted ordinary services.

During the killings, I chose not to pray to God. I sensed that it was not appropriate to involve Him in that. This choice came up naturally. Still, when dread would grip me suddenly in the night, if I had done too much during the day, I would ask God as a personal favor to let me stop for just a few days.

God preserved us from genocide until the crash of the president's plane; afterward He allowed Satan to win the match. That is my point of view. Since it was Satan who pushed us into this predicament, it is God alone who can judge us and punish us, not men, who are surpassed by the power of those other two, especially in this unnatural situation.

I know that only God can understand what we did. He alone has looked at every detail, He alone knows who drenched his arms and who did not. And regarding those last, it will not take Him long to count them up.

IGNACE: The white priests took off at the first skirmishes. The black priests joined the killers or the killed. God kept silent, and the churches stank from abandoned bodies. Religion could not find its place in our activities. For a little while, we were no longer ordinary Christians, we had to forget our duties learned in catechism class. We had first of all to obey our leaders—and God only afterward, very long afterward, to make confession and penance. When the job was done.

PANCRACE: In the marshes, pious Christians became ferocious killers. In prison, very ferocious killers became very pious Christians. But there are also pious Christians who became timid killers and timid killers who became quite pious Christians.

It happened for no clear reason. Each person satisfied his faith in his own way without any particular instructions, since the priests were gone or were up to their necks in it. In any case, religion adapted to these changes in belief.

ÉLIE: God and Satan seem quite contrasting in the Bible and the priest's sermons. The first one blazes with white and gold, the second with red and black. But in the marshes, the colors were those of muddy swamps and rotting leaves. It was as if God and Satan had agreed to cloud our eyes. I mean that we did not give a damn for either of them.

Once we found a little group of Tutsis in the papyrus. They were awaiting the machete blows with prayers. They did not plead with us, they did not ask us for mercy or even for a painless death. They said nothing to us. They did not even seem to be addressing heaven. They were praying and psalming among themselves. We made fun of them, we laughed at their *Amens*, we taunted them about the kindness of the Lord, we joked about the paradise awaiting them. That fired us up even more. Now the memory of those prayers just gnaws at my heart.

PIO: In the marshes, you heard no children's cries, not even murmurs. They waited silently in the mud. It was really something. When we uncovered a woman with a nursling, the infant would never even whimper. It was miraculous, so to speak.

Many Tutsis no longer asked to be spared, that was how they greeted death, among themselves. They had stopped hoping, they knew they had no chance for mercy and went off without a single prayer. They knew they were abandoned by everything, even by God. They no longer spoke to Him at all. They were leaving in suffering to join Him and no longer asked Him for anything, not comfort, not blessing, not welcome. They no longer prayed even to drive away the fear of an agonizing death.

It was too astounding, it was unnatural! Even animals that know nothing of pity, nothing of anguish, nothing of evil—they cry out terribly at the moment of the fatal blow.

That mystery drove us to many discussions. We sought explanations for these Tutsis who went off into death without breaking their silence. That could frighten us sometimes, at night, because it was said that such calmness must be a bad omen from heaven.

JOSEPH-DÉSIRÉ: Me, I was born Hutu, I did not choose this, it was God. I massacred some Tutsis, and then the Tutsis killed some Hutus. I have lost everything, except my life, for the moment. I no longer recognize my own existence in this chaos. It is God alone who can see it, watch over it, and guide it.

After all, what is there to say? There are some who killed and now thrive on their hills or in a villa abroad, others who killed and now sweat in the prison yard of those condemned to death. Why did God direct some toward happiness and others to the ordeal of suffering? Me, I don't know. I find myself here, in the purgatory of prison, but I still draw breath thanks to the power of God. I fear my capital punishment above everything else. We all fear dying before our day, since we remain human whatever the circumstances. That is why I have chosen to entrust my fate to God. He is the only one who could stop a genocide, He is the only one who can understand me, He is the only one who can save my life now. No human being can step between Him and me. That is what I want to believe from this moment on.

LÉOPORD: We no longer considered the Tutsis as humans or even as creatures of God. We had stopped seeing the world as it is, I mean as an expression of God's will.

That is why it was easy for us to wipe them out. And why those of us who prayed in secret did so for themselves, never for their victims. They prayed to ask for their crimes to be a bit forgotten, or to get just a little forgiveness—and they returned to the marshes in the morning.

Anyway, it was more than forbidden to speak kindly of the Tutsis to God or anyone else. Even after their deaths, even of a newborn. Even a priest was not to profit from his favor with God to pray for the soul of a Tutsi. He risked too much if someone overheard.

JEAN-BAPTISTE: Only dogs and wild beasts ventured into the church and its slaughterhouse stench. When we walked alongside the parish wall to go to Kanzenze or down into the marshes, that stink turned us even farther away from reading the gospels.

Truly, the times no longer wanted us to worry about God, and we went along. Deep down we knew that Christ was not on our side in this situation, but since He was not saying anything through the priests' mouths, that suited us.

ÉLIE: All the important people turned their backs on our killings. The blue helmets, the Belgians, the white directors, the black presidents, the humanitarian people and the international cameramen, the priests and the bishops, and finally even God. Did He watch what was happening in the marshes? Why did He not stab our murderous eyes with His wrath? Or show some small sign of disapproval to save more lucky ones? In those horrible moments, who could hear His silence? We were abandoned by all words of rebuke.

On Sunday mornings the radio programs no longer broadcast masses as before. But encouraging hearsay came from well-known monsignors who arrived from Kigali. Sometimes we heard hymns and services on the radio. Those were tapes without sermons, but the religious music soothed people who felt uneasy. It reminded them of ordinary Sundays—it did them some good.

JEAN-BAPTISTE: We could not ask time to give us a firm deadline for such a long program. Time seemed to smile on us, desiring only that we no longer worry about God. So we obeyed, and we kept on killing, aiming for the last one. Even though the work went on and on because of the looting and the fatigues of drinking, we never doubted, since no one could stop the work. But God slipped in among the killings to hurry along the *inkotanyi*. In the end God did not accept a definitive conclusion—that's the lesson.

Marie-Chantal: "Now, the guiltier the killers feel, the more they go to church. Likewise, the more traumatized the survivors feel, the more they go to church. Guilty ones and victims sit shoulder to shoulder praying in the first pew as if they had forgotten. Before the war, religion was not feverish as it is now. Now, many cling to prayers and hymns to get through this shattered life. Many preachers are pleased with this state of affairs. Even if there are no charitable feelings among those praying, there are no troublesome feelings in the churches. There is no fear, as on the hills.

"The less people look at one another with understanding and support, the more they gaze with love at the religious figures on the walls.

"As to Joseph-Désiré, I had thought he might well be killed at some point because of his actions. But prison forever, that, no. So we exchange Bible verses copied onto paper slips, thanks to visiting families, because we do not find much to say to each other about our new predicament."

Clémentine: "On their way to Congo, the Hutus carried into

exile the burden of the vanquished and the accursed. Some said the exile was a punishment from heaven, some said the punishment should be more painful. They fled along the roads with shame and terror at their heels. In the camps in Congo, they felt threatened on all sides and also by God. They feared ordinary and extraordinary retribution. They believed that the unnatural things they had done with their machetes would bring down upon them an equally unnatural chastisement."

LÉOPORD: Through killing well, eating well, looting well, we felt so puffed up and important, we didn't even care about the presence of God. Those who say otherwise are half-witted liars. Some claim today that they sent up prayers during the killings. They're lying: no one ever heard an *Ave Maria* or the like, they're only trying to jump in front of their colleagues on line for repentance.

In truth, we thought that from then on we could manage for ourselves without God. The proof—we killed even on Sunday without ever noticing it. That's all.

IN THE SHADE OF
AN ACACIA

We arrive in Rilima early in the morning, after the water chores, often bringing along some prisoners' relatives who load up the vehicle with bags of flour. We park beside the outer wall, on a road where inmates assigned to maintenance or book-keeping go about their work. The road is lined with gardens and detached houses accommodating some storerooms and the offices and lodgings of prison personnel. The little house at the end is a day-care center for the offspring of female prisoners, children conceived in captivity—through promiscuous happenstance or through more or less happy complicity.

A guard is waiting for us, always the same one, who writes down the names of the two people whom we wish to interview that day. While he goes to get them, we briefly greet the warden, his staff, some guards and trusties. I carefully stay away from any visiting prosecutors and lawyers, to avoid arousing suspicions among the prisoners. Innocent, a nervous and excitable soul, is constantly running into innumerable acquaintances, both impris-oned and free, with whom he simply must strike up endless discussions.

The conversations with the prisoners are individual and con-fidential, and not only with regard to the outside world. Nothing of what is said by one is ever reported to any of the others in the gang, not even to obtain further information about an event. This promise was a sine qua non—to prevent them from colluding on their stories beforehand and to avoid response strategies like those used in their testimony in court.

If a persistent misunderstanding or block occurs, the whole gang gets together, and we talk about the problem.

When the two prisoners arrive in their pink uniforms (styled as pajamas, suits, or Bermuda shorts, depending on the inmate's taste), we distribute the day's packages. We exchange confidences, anecdotes, and rumors—about the prison, the hills, Nyamata, the country at large, and what the radio is saying. Then we get settled in the garden of a prison house with our first interviewee while the other waits his turn in a neighboring garden, taking advantage of the open air and quiet to rest or gossip with pals, far from the crowd in the prison yard.

We sit face to face on two benches, by a hedge, in the shade of an acacia with drooping branches weighed down by many nests of yellow-and-black weaverbirds,★ whose squawks discourage eavesdropping. When the tape recorder is turned on, the interview begins, in French, or in Kinyarwanda (the Rwandan language) translated by Innocent.

On this subject, readers might well question the influence of the translator on the distinctive language of the speakers. Innocent understood that a transcription of the recorded material *in extenso* was the necessary first step, from oral to written oral testimony. I have to say that he then translated the testimony given in Kinyarwanda so faithfully and so well that it is impossible, even for a French-speaking Rwandan, to distinguish between the tran-

---

★*These avian artists live in colonies; a single tree may hold dozens of nests. Each nest is harmoniously spherical, delicately suspended, and set swaying by the slightest breath of air—a masterpiece of weaving. A colony of several thousand weaverbirds reigns supreme in the trees around the penitentiary in Rilima.*

scriptions that were translated and those made directly from spoken French.

Irrespective of the speaker, the language, the subject, or the mood of the day, each interview lasts about two hours. At that point either Innocent shows signs of understandable anger or I become exasperated or—most often—disgust, boredom, or frustration destroys both his concentration and mine. In short, we get tired. We feel the need, sometimes suddenly, to escape the universe into which our interviewee has plunged us with his imperturbable voice.

The prisoner, however, remains equably alert and receptive no matter what subject is raised and what turn the discussion takes, and he often seems disappointed or sorry when there is an interruption. Receptivity does not mean volubility. But while sometimes he may confine himself to an open-ended silence or cling stubbornly to an absurd lie, he never seems weary or displeased. In itself, his way of speaking, almost in a monotone, is radically different from that of the survivors.

It would be unthinkable to compare the accounts of the survivors with those of the killers, but one can briefly compare their manner of speaking.

Whenever I started a taped conversation with a survivor, it was always the beginning of something completely unpredictable. The dialogue might last five minutes or five hours. It was often interrupted by tears, untranslatable silences, disgressions—sometimes trivial and lighthearted—about daily life, or reflections on the war or agriculture; it might be punctuated by the arrival of visitors, the whims of a child, a Primus, a stroll, or a car ride.

Sometimes the survivor, man or woman, would offer several different versions of the same event from one day to the next.

This was usually for a reason that Angélique Mukamanzi, a young woman from Kanzenze, tactfully explained: "There are also people who constantly change the details of a fateful day because they believe that, on that day, their life snatched away the luck from another life that was just as worthy. Still, in spite of these zigzags, a person's memories do not go away . . . People choose certain memories, depending on their character, and they relive them as if they had happened just last year and will go on for another hundred years."

Or for another reason described by Janvier Munyaneza, a herdsman and *lycée* student in Kibungo: "Over time I sense that my mind sorts through my memories as it pleases, and I can't do anything about it—it's the same for my colleagues. Certain episodes are told over and over, so they expand with all the contributions from different people. They remain transparent, so to speak . . . Other episodes are neglected, and darken like a dream . . . But I know we no longer have any interest in inventing or exaggerating or concealing, as we did at the liberation, because we are no longer muddled by fear of the machetes."

In every case, it was easy to speak frankly about these "zigzags." Sometimes the survivor might break off abruptly, because, in the words of Marie-Louise Kagoyire, a shopkeeper in Nyamata, "showing our hearts to a stranger, talking about how we feel, laying bare our feelings as survivors is shocking beyond measure. When the exchange of words becomes too blunt, as in this moment with you, one must come to a full stop."

On the other hand, we went through several nice, polite, but discouraging meetings with Francine Niyitegeka, a farmer and shopkeeper in Kibungo, before she said at last, "Fine—if you come tomorrow, we'll talk." She had finally managed to work through a psychological blockage and went on to speak about how the marshes had destroyed the bond between her and her fi-ancé in these terms: "We had no intimacy left. We felt too scat-tered, we couldn't find real words to exchange, or gestures of kindness for touching each other. I mean, if we met, it no longer mattered to either of us, since we each worried more than any-thing else about saving our own life."

It was harrowing to see the risks these survivors took in telling their stories. They did not hesitate to let themselves be overwhelmed by their memories, their uneasiness, their pain. They dared to revisit forbidden places and to bring nightmares back to life. Quite often they spoke of memories and thoughts they had never revealed before, and seemed astonished at what they or others had said. They whispered, flared up, became harsh or tender. The tone of their voices was never the same from one day to the next. Even if their stories changed in the telling, you had to listen to them with all your heart.

But the killers never allow themselves to be overwhelmed by anything. Their memories may fool them because of normal de-formations over time, but that is nothing like the traumas and psychological blocks their victims have described.

Each killer controls what he says in his own way. Élie, for ex-ample, tries touchingly to express his feelings as precisely as pos-sible, while Ignace automatically answers at first with a lie that he can then carefully refine. All of them gradually speak more sin-cerely as the interviews progress, making more of an effort to open up. Nevertheless, there is a cautionary line that they almost always refuse to cross. Although they speak in a monotone that increases our uneasiness, there is something more, something equivocal in their voices that makes us think these men are not so indifferent as they appear. Their guardedness is dictated probably by prudence or perplexity, often by a strange insensitivity, but also perhaps by a sense of propriety. It is worth remembering that since their return to Rwanda they have not yet met any survivors face to face. We shall get back to this later.

Finally, we might mention the question of vocabulary. To describe events, the survivors employed a vocabulary that was raw, vivid, and precise. They constantly used the words *job*, *cutting*, or *pruning*, taken from the work on banana plantations, to designate the murderous action of the machete. Said Jeannette Ayinkamiye, "I know that when you have seen your mama cut so cruelly . . . you lose forever some of your trust in others. I mean, you will never again be able to live with people as you did before." Or Berthe Mwanankabandi: "Others could not help making a last gesture to ward off the machete that would cut them, a gesture that would make them suffer even more. This refusal is our bond with nature."

Moreover, they all spoke of the genocide—using this new word in their language, *itfembabwoko*, or falling back on the word *ubwicanyi*, "killing"—with an astonishing grasp of its significance.

Jeannette: "When there has been one genocide there can be another, at any time in the future, anywhere—if the cause is still there and no one knows what it is."

Édith Uwanyiligira: "During the genocide, survivors lose their confidence along with everything else, and that muddles them more than they realize. They can doubt everything—strangers, colleagues, even their surviving neighbors . . . Understand this: the genocide will not fade from our minds. Time will hold on to the memories, it will never spare more than a tiny place for the solace of the soul."

Innocent: "Genocide is not really a matter of poverty or lack of education . . . In 1959 the Hutus relentlessly robbed, killed, and drove away Tutsis, but they never for a single day imagined exterminating them. It is the intellectuals who emancipated them, by planting the idea of genocide in their heads and sweeping away their hesitations."

Berthe: "Genocide pushes into isolation those who were not pushed into death."

Sylvie: "I must make clear that after a genocide, certain words no longer have their old meaning, certain words just lose their meaning, and anyone who listens must watch out for the changes."

The killers, on the other hand, use the word *genocide* rarely and only when alluding to the responsibility of the authorities, the directives from the capital and from the people in charge—in other words, only in relation to others, never when speaking of the events in which they themselves were protagonists. For that they prefer instead the word *itsembatsemba*, "massacres," and especially *intambara*, "war," thus likening their actions to the wars of previous generations or in other African countries.

"Basically," explains Innocent, "if they sometimes use that word *genocide* in an answer, it's just from inattention, because you used it in the question and they can't think of another one fast enough. Otherwise, they avoid it as a troublesome word. They classify their memories as routine killings. Deep down they're not interested in the word, only in the penalties it might bring." In the same way, the killers almost never say "survivor" (*rescapé*), preferring to use words like "a stricken person," "someone who has suffered" (*personne éprouvée*), or "survivor" (*survivant*).★

Continuing this logic, during our first meetings the killers try to use military language to describe their actions. Pancrace Hakizamungili, who sometimes seems like the most cynical or indifferent member of the gang, boldly announces: "Then began the

---

★*The French terms for "survivor" distinguish between someone who has escaped from a calamity such as an earthquake, plane crash, or massacre, un rescapé, and someone who has survived disaster on a smaller or a more personal scale, un survivant. —Translator's note.*

terrible battle of the marshes." The excessively pious Fulgence Bunani informs us, "We usually made war with machetes because we had no other weapons." Encountering our disbelief or irritation, they rapidly abandon that tactic to return to a more realistic vocabulary. They say that they "hit" or "cut."

To conclude these lexicological remarks, here is an anecdote that illustrates both the killers' state of mind and the above-mentioned necessity to do these interviews with a group of people, not with isolated individuals.

During the first meetings, the men deny everything with placid obstinacy whenever they are questioned about their own participation: they have not personally done anything or seen anything, period. Innocent and I are stupefied by their aplomb. Above all, we cannot understand the contradiction between their much-debated collective agreement to talk to us and the unbelievable denials that pour out when they do start talking. After much discussion and growing disappointment, I begin to think that my project is in fact unrealizable, although I remain mystified by their repeated assurances of cooperation, since they don't have that much to gain from our undertaking except a little relaxation in a shady garden.

The key to the mystery arrives by chance when, without realizing it, I sometimes pass from the informal, singular "you" (*tu*) to the plural "you" (*vous*). Each time, as if by magic, the replies become precise, and I finally grasp the link between cause and effect.

For example, to the question, "Can you (*tu*) describe how you (*tu*) would begin your mornings?" they would answer, "I would get up, I would go to the field to cut the sorghum and count the goats." But to the question, "Can you (*tu*) describe how you (*vous*) would begin your mornings?" they would answer, "We would get up at dawn, we would gather on the soccer field at around nine o'clock . . . Then we would go down to the marshes and search the papyrus using the machetes."

In fact, although each one is willing to recount, on his own, his experience of the genocide, they all feel the need to hide behind a more diluted syntax, to replace "I" by a more collective, impersonal "we." To broach certain very personal subjects, such as "The First Time" or "And God in All This?" I wait for our moments of greatest complicity, which often come at the end of our meetings, when we have grown used to one another.

REMORSE AND REGRETS

ADALBERT: I often have the same dream: I see the fields, the euca-lyptus along the roads, the banana trees in front of my house. I dream longingly of green plantations I have not seen again since the genocide. I dream of my home in Kibungo, of the forests, the banana groves, and the river there, and the coolness in the shade, without anyone to crowd or aggravate me.

But as to daydreams or persistent memories, what comes to mind are only those from the first days, when it was still new for me to kill Tutsis. The other memories, the daily expeditions that followed, have been worn away by habit.

FULGENCE: You do not forget anything that happened during the killings. The details are truly there when you want to dip into them. Still, certain colleagues tend to remember the grim and unfortunate moments, while others recall the good times, like the comfort and abundance. Me, I don't rid myself of the serious memories; I regret misjudging events and I regret the people who were killed. I thought wrong, I went wrong, I did wrong. An evil is spoiling my life, and my days are steeped in misery.

Those dead people and those acts of killing do not invade my dreams, however; in any case, they leave me with no horrible im-ages when I wake up. Night is never a scolding thing, except when I wake in darkness. I can feel shivery then. I don't know why—whether it is from the pain of a bad bed or the idea of my prison future.

IGNACE: I think time will allow me to leave the difficult memories behind in Rilima, when I get to leave. I will fold the bad thoughts up inside the prison uniform. I think I will go home with my memory in fine shape, to pick up life again in good spirits.

But the memory of the mine shaft where the Tutsis were smoked alive, that one will never leave me. I can feel it well hidden behind my mind. It will eat at me on the hill. And that is a big thing. It is going to stalk me with no warning, since I live not far from the mines.

I had not foreseen that this memory would work at me so viciously. I believe it is because of the smell of the burns—I believe it is unnatural for men to kill men with fire.

ALPHONSE: In my dreams I revisit scenes of bloody hunting and looting. Sometimes, though, it is actually me who gets the machete blow and wakes up shaking. He wants to cut me and bleed me out. I try to see who is striking me, but my fear hides the face of the man who wishes me harm. I do not know if he is Hutu or Tutsi, a neighbor or an *inkotanyi*. I would like to know if he is a victim, to ask pardon of his family and hope for peace of mind that way, but the sleeping man refuses.

My wife said that I would have a drunkard's regrets, that I drank so much and killed so much that I would never know either who or how many they were. Me, it is first of all that man I would like to know about. He's the one to whom I must propose an offer of peace.

That dream torments me—but not often. On the contrary, it's mostly this wretched prison life that cuts into my sleep.

I believe we are all the same at night. Our own misfortunes take over our nightmares more easily than the misfortunes of others. Our sufferings as prisoners push other people's hardships out of the way, both day and night, I see no mystery in that. I think my sleep will recover a normal restfulness when I regain my liberty and the life I used to have.

JEAN-BAPTISTE: I often dream I am walking in freedom on the road to Ntarama. I go along, among the familiar trees. I feel refreshed and at ease, and I am content. I wake up full of nostalgia on my pallet.

Other nights dreaming tips into calamity. I see again the people I killed with my own hand. When that happens, every awful detail of blood and terror comes back: the mud, the heat of the chase, the colleagues . . . Only the cries are missing. These are silent killings, which seem slow but are as dreadful as before. My dreams in prison are of various kinds, sometimes somber, sometimes calm; perhaps they flow from the various situations of my life here, whether I am sick or in good health. Who can tell if they will change when I get out? My hope is they'll forget about me.

All the prisoners live unhappily since the genocide. Many complain about their fate, but not to the point of turning to a deadly remedy. I know of no one driven by remorse or nightmares to extreme measures. I know of no case of suicide in prison during my seven years here. There are a dozen cases of people eating filth, tearing their clothes, writhing on the ground, or screaming in waking dreams—but raving enough to take their own lives, never.

PIO: Night sometimes takes me back to the soccer field, where nostalgia is waiting for me. I dream I am meeting other players on the team, those who are dead and those who are scattered. I played with the number nine on my back—I was a striker, with a lot of speed and a hard shot. When I wake up, I still think for a moment that the game will go on . . . After I leave prison, I hope we'll get soccer going again among those who are still alive, to draw closer together. The rest of my dreams slide easily from memory, and they no longer bother me.

Memories are more wrenching than dreams. In Rilima, there are some who pretend not to remember anything because they fear punishment—here below or up above. They relate details of life after or even before the killings, but never during, or they just mention things of no account.

They cheat, they cheat with themselves trying to win that game. They are playacting a kind of madness. They forget their misfortunes and find it convenient to fool themselves that way. But I've met no one sincerely crazy enough to have truly forgotten that he killed.

In the Tutsi camp it must be quite different. I do not know about their situation, but I think this madness might well exist in those who escaped the killings. Those who shared life with a number of the dead . . . I mean those who watched numerous raids while awaiting their turns, who expected to fall bathed in blood into the last darkness—their reason might crumble. Insanity comes more from experiencing evil, and the suffering it brings, than from inflicting them.

I don't forget the terrible things I did. I do forget names, days, situations; I try to forget painful moments so as to hold on to peaceful ones. But there's no hope of success in the long run, regarding the hunts in the marshes . . . I have a feeling that remorse is determined not to assuage my memory.

JOSEPH-DÉSIRÉ: I don't dream about anything in particular, not the massacres, not the camps in Congo. I mean, none of my dreams ever get repeated. Sleep leaves hardly any room for visiting my past.

My death sentence—I think about that every day, of course. The subject comes up daily among us, since all the condemned prisoners are crowded into the same block. In spite of everything, the sentence never jumps out at me in dreams, though, and neither does fear, which lies in wait for me only when I wake up.

My sleep and those who visit it have hardly changed in Rilima. I still dream of unknown things, of things I can imagine without going near them, such as things I want. For example, after your visits, perhaps I will dream I am traveling to France, to Paris, where I have never been.

PANCRACE: In prison, malaria and cholera have taken a heavy toll. Fear of vengeance has killed. The miserable life here and the fights have killed, but regrets—never. Life proves too vigorous against regrets and the like.

Someone who killed too much in the marshes tends to abandon his bloodstained memories among the corpses he left behind. He wants only to remember the little he did in the marshes that everyone saw and that he cannot deny without being called a liar. He hides the rest. He mislays remorse that is too damaging. His memory serves his own interest, it zigzags to guide him through the risks of punishment.

Clémentine: "Me, I see that the survivors and the killers do not remember the same way at all.

"If the killers agree to speak up, they are able to tell the truth in every detail about what they did. They have kept a more normal memory of what happened on their hill. Their memory doesn't bump up against anything they've lived, it doesn't feel overwhelmed by horrible events. It is never mired in confusion. The killers keep their memories in clear water. But they share these memories only among themselves, because they are risky.

"The survivors do not get along so well with their memories, which zigzag constantly with the truth, because of fear or the humiliation of what happened to them. Survivors feel they are to blame in a different way. They feel more to blame in a certain sense for a transgression that will always be beyond them. For them, the dead are near, even touching them. Survivors must get together in little groups to add up and compare their memories, taking careful steps, making no mistakes. Then afterward they will recall the dire events without fear of ambush.

"Survivors seek tranquillity in one part of memory. The killers look for it in another part. Killers and survivors share neither sadness nor fear. They do not ask for the same kind of help from falsehood. I think they will never be able to share an important part of the truth."

ÉLIE: When I dream of those times, it is my wife who appears, and the field, and the house, but almost never the killed people. Except for the social worker, of course, because she was the first one I struck down. Basically my dreams try to slip past those moments of killing.

In memories, on the other hand, it is a big deal: those moments track me and often catch up with me.

I know colleagues who hope to escape their crimes by forgetting them. Some prisoners here in Rilima claim that by trying hard not to remember, you can manage to forget. I don't think so, not where I am concerned, in any case. A memory of killing gets by, it adapts to lies, it comes and goes, but it does not wash out.

No prisoner has paid for his remorse with his life. Not one has even tried or faked that to win a little pity. In prison, death has come with the epidemics, and with the infernal misery of the place, but never with feelings of shame and suchlike.

IGNACE: It is just as damaging to tell the truth to the justice system, to the population, or to yourself.

Even in your heart of hearts, it is riskier to remember than to forget. Therefore I try to keep quiet with myself. The time will come to hear the truth about these things surpassing ordinary crimes.

In prison, some are waiting for a change in their situation to start up again. They see themselves as too crushed at present to show any regrets. They say that after all they have lost, it's not worth it, that they have walked too long in one direction, machete in hand, to go back—where nothing good awaits them. They say that memories only bring troubles. The only way they see themselves winning is by succeeding the next time, and for good.

ADALBERT: I knew my misdeeds would come to light when I returned from Congo. But I chose to bring my offenses back to my local penitentiary rather than to hide them in the Congo jungle, with no acquaintances to share them. I don't know if my repentance will be accepted, if I will be spared. But penitence is like death: you must bring it back home to your hill.

Gaspard, a survivor: "If killers come to church to pray to God on their knees, to show us their remorse, I cannot pray either with them or against them. Real regrets are said eye to eye, not to statues of God. The accommodation of killers is not my concern."

ÉLIE: In prison and on the hills, everyone is obviously sorry. But most of the killers are sorry they didn't finish the job. They accuse themselves of negligence rather than wickedness. Those who keep saying that they weren't there during the fatal moments, that they don't remember a thing, that they lost their machetes and tripe like that, they are bowing down with the hope of evading punishment—while waiting to start all over again. Repentance may wear many faces. But it is worthless if it is not the right kind.

LÉOPORD: Some try to show remorse but tremble before the truth. They sneak around it, because of too many conflicting interests, and wind up flung backward.

It was in a camp in Congo that I first felt my heart ache. I prayed, hoping to find relief, but in vain. After prayers or hymns, shame waited for me, without fail. So I began being sorry out loud, paying no attention to the mockery spewing from my comrades' mouths. In prison I told my whole truth. It came out freely. Ever since then, whenever someone asks me for it, it flows the same way.

Aside from this vile prison life, I have felt calm since I spoke up. I'm waiting peacefully to go home to my land. I do not fear any problem returning to work in the fields beside the neighbors on the hill. On the contrary, I am impatient for my next life.

Marie-Chantal: "The culprit and the victim will ask forgetfulness for a little protection. It won't be for the same reason. And they will not be asking for it together. But they will appeal to the very same forgetfulness."

JOSEPH-DÉSIRÉ BITERO

Dry, dusty air weighed heavily on the prison one morning. Blazing heat marked every face and slowed the usual bustle in the road of houses near the outer wall, except, of course, for the fluttering of the weaverbirds busily braiding their globular nests. I observed those delicate masterpieces dangling from the tips of the acacia branches while I waited for Joseph-Désiré Bitero and mulled over the surprising remark Innocent had just made about him, in the car: "At heart, that one was really a jolly guy, who smiled at everything and nothing. He enjoyed meeting people. He was nice. He'd share a drink and conversation with any comrade at all."

Joseph-Désiré Bitero had not been invited to the first discussions I had with the group because I was afraid his authority as a former local *interahamwe* leader, plus his aura and status as a prisoner condemned to death, might increase the group's misgivings. So, I knew him only by reputation, but many people had spoken about him.

Shadowed by a tall, thin soldier, Joseph-Désiré Bitero arrived in his pink uniform with a swing in his step, exchanging discreet friendly greetings with every other prisoner he met. I understood Innocent's remark immediately: Joseph-Désiré, the center of attention, was smiling. He did seem jolly, said hello nicely, and would gladly have offered us a beer if he'd had one handy.

Unlike most of the others in the gang, Joseph-Désiré was

born into a family with local roots going back several generations, on the hill of Kanazi, a half-hour from Nyamata. His parents, he says, "were good farmers. They were neither well off nor badly off. They simply made a decent living."

Decent enough to encourage him to continue his studies beyond the primary level and to take the competitive examinations for teachers' training college. "I was a satisfactory student. It was not my decision to take the exams. In my day, the professors and your grades determined which students pursued which professions. In my case, fate chose teaching. When I was a child, I saw teachers as special people, honored at ceremonies, much listened to, well dressed—so admirable. I embraced my destiny without wavering."

Joseph-Désiré cannot remember anything noteworthy about his childhood with his three brothers and four sisters. "Those years gave me the life of an ordinary little boy. Sickness spared me, school welcomed me, there was enough to eat, I took up the hoe during the rainy season to help out the family. I liked to play soccer and watch the games, too. I lived in the house where I was born and where I expected to die."

Later, he added this one observation: "I was raised in the fear that the *mwami*—the Tutsi kings—and their commanders might return; that was because of all the stories old folks told us at home about unpaid forced labor and other humiliations of that sad period for us, and because of the awful things happening to our brothers in Burundi." Born in 1961, two years after the abolition of the Tutsi monarchy, young Joseph-Désiré grew up in an atmosphere where the hostility to Tutsis was exacerbated by the influx of refugees from Burundi, but he tacitly admits that there was no real fear of tragedy in the region.

Joseph-Désiré received his diploma and became a tall, strapping young man. He married a pretty neighbor from his childhood, Marie-Chantal Munkaka, who bore him three children. He took an interest in politics early on, much earlier than his pals, certainly through the influence of his cousin Bernard, the burgomaster of Nyamata. "When I wanted to join a party, there was only one: the MRND.* It was the party of President Habyarimana, the burgomaster, civil servants, and Hutus like me. After other parties appeared, it never occurred to me to change. I preached the ideas of the president, which seemed most profitable for my Hutu brothers, the ideas that addressed the threat of rebels and of oppositionist political figures. I figured those ideas would prevail because of our majority, the army, and government negotiations. That suited me fine.

"With the new multiparty situation," he adds, "squabbles broke out, at first with the other Hutu groups. Things got serious among us. The local Tutsis, on the other hand, kept their distance from political feuds. They minded their own business and voiced no troublesome opinions."

This was a significant admission, because Joseph-Désiré Bitero's first victims, in fact, were not Tutsis but Hutus from two extremes: pacifists, who favored dialogue with the rebels, and those who were hostile to any negotiations and supported an all-out war.

Joseph-Désiré can be believed when he affirms, "I was born surrounded by Tutsis in Kanazi. I always had Tutsi acquaintances and thought nothing of it. Still, I did grow up listening to history lessons and radio programs that were always talking about major problems between Hutus and Tutsis—though I lived among Tutsis who posed no problem. The situation was going to pieces due to the impossible gap between the worrisome news about the

---

*Mouvement national révolutionnaire pour le développement, or National Revolutionary Movement for Development, founded in 1975. (In 1991 "revolutionary" was changed to "republican.")

mess on the country's borders and the peaceful people who lived next door. The situation was bound to come apart and to go into either savagery or neighborliness."

The fact remains that Joseph-Désiré's political engagement was from the beginning zealous and deeply committed. Why this sudden infatuation? the excitement of nascent ambition? the enjoyment or release of an excess of physical strength? the pleasures of power and organization? self-interest? It's difficult to say.

Let's simply note that there is no evidence of any event in his childhood, any cause of humiliation or resentment, which might have fed a personal desire for revenge, and that for a young teacher, climbing the social ladder but living on a meager salary, this party in power for twenty-five years, the party of his cousin the burgomaster, was the only pathway to success—unless he tried his luck in the capital or in the army, which was risky for a farmer's son who had never set foot outside Nyamata.

He himself puts it this way: "It was an absorbing activity that could bring small advantages. We had a good time at the formal political events. We wanted the superiority of power and all its satisfactions."

Joseph-Désiré impressed everyone with his imposing presence at meetings and his relaxed good humor in *cabarets*. He bought a modest house built of fired brick in Gatare, the Nyamata neighborhood favored by educated people and civil servants. His wife, Marie-Chantal, found a position at the maternity hospital. On any given day, with the same easygoing manner, Joseph-Désiré would spend time both with Tutsi pals and with rabidly anti-Tutsi Hutu fanatics.

Talking about the Bitero he knew back then, Innocent says: "Basically, Bitero started out a good guy, well spoken, who did not seem at all dangerous. He had no thought of doing harm. Aside from his being in the other camp, it was fun to pop a bottle with him. Without the tumult of war, he might have remained the man he was."

For Joseph-Désiré, the tumult began in 1991, when the *inkotanyi* attacks and the political wrangling led to a vast increase in public virulence, and new orators began crisscrossing the country. It was then that Joseph-Désiré discovered the joys of militancy in his party's youth groups. "My job was to enroll young Hutus, to keep them from going astray into crime or into the wrong parties," he explains. "I urged them to listen to the president's speeches; I organized gymnastic exercises, games, and meetings to explain our policies. But the war took a wrong turn. The Rwandan army could not hold the front, and we suspected a cover-up of their defeat. That fanned the politicians' brutality and thirst for vengeance. We militants were intoxicated by orders, and we acquiesced."

The word "acquiesced" is a euphemism, because two years later, in 1993, Joseph-Désiré was elected president of the party's youth organization. "I don't know why people elected me. I don't know what they saw in me. I think they felt confident because I was educated and very eager. They knew I never hung back." The presidency entailed specific duties, including leadership of the town's militias, the *interahamwe*—a word Joseph-Désiré has a hard time saying. "It's too complicated, because the meaning of the word *interahamwe* shifted in the time between my nomination and the massacres. When I accepted, I had no thought of killing, except perhaps if a pressing need arose. I mean, I had no thought of killing for killing's sake."

True? false? When did that idea germinate? When did it take root? He lies in response to this last question, since he denies all premeditation before the assassination of President Habyarimana. "His death shook us up, panic drove us into the killings, and I found myself right in the middle of the genocide."

Among accounts of this gestation period, the one given by Christine—a native of Kanazi, like her neighbor Joseph-Désiré—is categorical: "In the *cabarets*, men had begun talking about massacres in 1992. I remember clearly, because of the uproar around the political parties. After the new parties first met, *interahamwe* committees sprang up in the communes, and the current was shut off between us. The president of Nyamata commune was Joseph-Désiré. He visited all the Hutu homes, explained the threat of the *inkotanyi* from Uganda, and checked to see that the tools behind sacks of beans were well sharpened. I remember distinctly because one day his foot tipped over the cooking pot in the courtyard—that was during the dry season before the killings."

In other words between December and March, which supports Innocent's point when he says of Joseph-Désiré: "From January on, three months before the genocide, his character was completely transformed. If I went into the local *cabaret* we both went to, he'd stop talking until I left. He knew perfectly well he was going to kill me."

Of all the men in the gang, Joseph-Désiré is the only one who concretely envisaged the genocide beforehand. Two months in advance, he began to examine the machetes. During the night after Habyarimana's assassination, he met with the functionaries of the town. On the first day of the killings, he was conspicuous in the main street, waving his machete, and then he led the way into the church.

Moreover, he admits, "I had the privilege of being a leader; I had to set a good example. I was eager for approval." During the next eight weeks he deployed his formidable energy everywhere at once: in the evening at organization meetings, in the morning in the Nyamwiza marshes, in the afternoon in Kibungo, in

Ntarama, or on the streets of Nyamata, talking, debating, arguing, enrolling all the local Adalberts and their gangs.

He did all this without neglecting his family or his wife, Marie-Chantal, who shares with us this heartwarming picture of a war criminal: "He came home often. He never carried a weapon, not even his machete. I knew he was a leader, I knew the Hutus were out there cutting Tutsis. With me, he behaved nicely. He made sure we had everything we needed. One day he even had his stepfather's second wife escorted to Kabgayi because she had Tutsi blood.

"Actually, he was steeped in bad politics but not in bad thoughts. He was gentle with the children. I did not want to ask him about the trouble that was spreading everywhere. To me, he was the nice man I married." She adds, "Today, when he sends a note from prison, he does not dwell on the change. He appears cheerful, makes no demands, sends advice and encouragement, hides his suffering."

To explain his return from Congo and the inevitable death sentence awaiting him, Joseph-Désiré says, "I knew about the overcrowded prisons, I knew many prisoners were dying. But I wanted to return to Rwanda so my family could get a chance for a normal life on our land. I didn't want my daughters to end up as dirty beggars in forests far from home."

His trial began two and a half years after his return, on May 26, 1998, in Nyamata. On the witness stand, Joseph-Désiré's attitude was stupid, odious, and untenable, yet rather bold and resolute.

He had pleaded guilty, but his confession hadn't been accepted because he denied the essential fact of his crimes, disclaimed responsibility for his actions, and said he was simply following orders. He showed no remorse about his victims, either, and during our interviews, he never once seemed to understand the monstrosity of his actions.

True, he did not beg for mercy or denounce anyone else in order to try to escape capital punishment. He simply trotted out his unacceptable arguments, some of which he repeated to us: "I was more implicated because I was more faithful to the party then . . . If I hadn't acted, it wouldn't have changed a thing, because everyone was in agreement, each in his own capacity. I tried my best to support what was considered the right thing to do at the time." Although it was hard to understand how he could be so defiant, he would not budge, and the hostile reception he had in the courtroom did not faze him. According to Innocent, "The public's reaction was heated, because he was a well-known *interahamwe*, and the survivors were especially upset, whereas he appeared calm, collected, and very much on guard."

His defense was hopeless, but different tactics would not have changed the verdict. He was tried alone and before any international or Rwandan government interventions were made in favor of a policy of reconciliation. His was a show trial for central Africa, one of the first opportunities to hear the testimony of survivors, to listen to their grief and to learn the facts. Among them was Innocent, who accused Joseph-Désiré of killing his wife and child in the church.

Of his trial, Joseph-Désiré observes: "Everything I said I would say again today. I was tried at a time when the survivors felt too much anger. They expected some kind of punishment, and the new authorities wanted to give them a spectacular revenge. Afterward I listened to the trial of Monsignor Misango on the radio. He was acquitted. The former secretary general of my party lives quietly at home. There is even a national organizer of the genocide who briefly became prime minister before fleeing to lead a busy life in America. That is how good and bad luck happen in one party. The thinkers got the genocide going, and the militants paid for the damage."

At one point in our interviews when Joseph-Désiré tries to present himself as a scapegoat, the expiatory victim of a politicized judicial system, Innocent interrupts brusquely and points out that someone who won't confess has no right to complain. I remind Joseph-Désiré that he was an educated person and the leader of killers. "I was a teacher," he replies. "I was a committed party member, I obeyed, I killed. In a party, a leader can't just do what he wants. Yes, I had a teaching diploma, but it wasn't for me to think about our activists' political slogans. That's not what you're there for when the situation gets hot. All I had to think about was implementation." Listening to him, you wonder if he doesn't actually believe what he is saying.

Whenever Joseph-Désiré goes back and forth between his special block and the garden by the road, he claps some former drinking or killing companion on the back, fires off a joke, winks and rolls his eyes, and asks how everyone's doing, testing his popularity while trying to renew old ties. He even attempts a genuine reconciliation with Innocent. He has few complaints about his cramped and unpleasant quarters, except that they're giving him rheumatism. He obeys the warden and guards without resentment or servility. The only help he requests is not for him but for his daughters, whom he will probably never see again. He tries constantly to turn our interviews into discussions about history or geopolitics in which his personal itinerary melts away.

"You will never see the source of a genocide," he says. "It is buried too deep in grudges, under an accumulation of misunderstandings that we were the last to inherit. We came of age at the worst moment in Rwanda's history: we were taught to obey absolutely, raised in hatred, stuffed with slogans. We are an unfortunate generation."

He also says, "There are situations that set you singing if you win or crying if you lose," an unwitting plagiarism of the same observation made by Robert Servatius, Adolf Eichmann's lawyer, at his trial in Jerusalem: "There are some actions for which you are decorated if you succeed and sent to the scaffold if you fail."

On April 24, 1998, the Rwandan government decreed the first—and so far the only—day of national example. On that day thirty-three people were executed in stadiums or other public places. Six prisoners were brought from Rilima to the hill of Kayumba, before a crowd of people who thought Joseph-Désiré was among the condemned, but he escaped that execution thanks to a delay in his trial. Two months later, after eight days in court, he was sentenced to death. Since then he has been waiting for a presidential pardon or Rwanda's abolition of the death penalty. He listens to the radio, he plays *igisoro*,* and he prays.

Of all the participants in the group, he is the only one who can imagine the possible consequences of a book about them being published abroad, and he secretly hopes that what he says in it will help to delay his execution. Then why not make an effort to tell the truth, which cannot harm him now in any case? Is he unwilling to try? incapable of trying? unable to distinguish anymore between what he wants others to believe and what he wants to believe? Has he wound up believing in his classic, repeated theme—obedience? His reply: "When the decision about the killings reached us, duty kept me from backing out. It was be-

---

*The Rwandan version of the ancient African game awele, as hard to win as it is easy to play. Igisoro is as popular in Rwanda as dominoes in Tunisia or chess in the Balkans.

yond difficult: things were rushing along too fast for us to think as we do today, six years later.

"For someone who had been recruited by politics," he adds, "the only choice was to run away or become an organizer. Run away? As I told you before, I never considered that. Or the possibility that the authorities had the wrong perspective. I told myself that if the job had to be done, it had to be done quickly and completely. When war threatens your land, when you can rely on the strength of the majority, of the party that's best for your intellectual and material well-being, and when you enjoy the confidence of the authorities, you do your utmost without counting the cost."

Without counting the victims? He doesn't wince at the question and says again, "We had lived with Tutsi friends without noticing it, and we became contaminated by ethnic racism without noticing it."

Then he finally says something that reveals the abyss of incomprehension lying between us: "If a divine miracle were to help me return to my hill, my family, and a job, people would see that I can become an ordinary person again."

THE ORGANIZERS

PANCRACE: Given the way things went after the president's plane crash, I think the genocide was organized down to the last detail by the intimidators in Kigali. On the hills, though, we were late in getting specific information about the killings. We were heating up, biding time, waiting for instructions, we didn't know what. Actually, we learned about the genocide after it had already started.

ALPHONSE: The day after the plane crash, the burgomaster of Nyamata came to Kanzenze with some policemen to hold an important meeting. He told us about the crash, he explained the flight of the Tutsis who thought they were under suspicion for our president's death, and he asked us to maintain order and security. But while he was speaking, some policemen and *interahamwe* were dragging their thumbs across their necks, as if cutting throats.

After the burgomaster left, a retired warrant officer announced very clearly, "All right, the burgo is gone, we'll go on patrol. Grab some clubs and machetes for safety's sake." Off we went. We roamed around the Tutsis' places, trading threats with them and some nasty, bloody blows, but we hardly cut at all because the Tutsis were still strong and staying together, and we were watching out not to get hurt.

That's how the first ones got started on the job, basically—without the authorities' permission.

JOSEPH-DÉSIRÉ: The platforms of all the Hutu political parties had been proposing Tutsi killings since 1992. Those agendas were descriptive and meticulous. They were read aloud at meetings and warmly applauded. They were read over the radio, especially after the Arusha accords. Everyone could easily learn about them and understand them, the whites and the Tutsis in particular.

In the town, we had got ready to begin new massacres to counter the *inkotanyi* attacks. We anticipated just the usual massacres, however, the kind we had known for thirty years. The more the *inkotanyi* pushed into the country, the more we would massacre their Tutsi brothers on their farms, to deter them and halt the advance: that was how we saw the situation at the municipal level. Regarding the genocide, we never received precise notification before the first day.

I had become involved in politics because of my cousin the burgomaster. We wanted the ideas of the president and the majority of Hutus to prevail. We wanted to wind up winners in every situation—that's normal practice among people who do politics, in a way. Except that the escalation of the war ran the ordinary routines of power into a ditch, so to speak, and left us disorganized.

The highest authorities corrupted a war based on grudges piled up since the Tutsi kings and turned it into a genocide. We were overwhelmed. We found ourselves faced with a done deal we had to get done, if I may put it that way. When the genocide came from Kigali, taking us by surprise, I never flinched. I thought, If the authorities opted for this choice, there's no reason to sidestep the issue.

Let us say that the chaotic situation had come to seem too natural to me. The things that went without saying, the obligations—it all happened so fast there was no room left for any kind of hesitation. You were either pushed into flight by cowardice or drawn to your machete by obedience.

Innocent: "Joseph-Désiré weaves his way through many lies, for he has never been a fool. I've known him since our school days, and we later became colleagues and friends since we were both teachers. When he was made president of the *interahamwe*, much feared and much renowned, we were in opposing camps, but that did not prevent us from sharing a Primus and some laughs.

"Still, as I said before, his character changed completely after January. If I came into our neighborhood *cabaret*, he'd stop talking until I left. If our paths crossed, he would change direction and look away; suddenly he began avoiding conversation with me, refusing all contact. We hadn't quarreled about anything, or fallen out over a hurtful word, but he had already expelled me from his circle. He preferred putting in hours at closed meetings with influential people. He was still friendly, but only to his Hutu compatriots.

"What I think now is that he didn't know the tiny details of the genocide, such as the day and the exact agenda. But he certainly knew three months in advance that he was going to kill me, and my wife and my child, with whom he had shared pleasant times. He was in on the secret of the genocide without knowing how it would operate.

"After his arrest, we ran into each other in court and I burst out at him: 'You, you knew everything for a long time and you never gave the slightest warning to save at least my wife! Maybe you even killed her with your own hands in the church.' He mouthed conciliatory words in response, but he dodged the answer."

ÉLIE: In 1991, after the first attacks from the rebels in Uganda, army newspapers singled out the Tutsi as the Hutu's natural enemy who had to be definitively destroyed. It was written in big fat letters on page one.

Afterward the targeting slowly spread by radio. At political meetings they instructed us to stop sharing land or goods with Tutsis, to stop intermarrying, or helping each other with farm work, or forgiving even a single thing in daily affairs. Because one day we'd set out to kill them, and these arrangements would hinder us. But as to the date and the means, we received no information.

Actually, the soldiers and civil servants thought the intimidators had decided to kill the Tutsis gradually, so as to discourage the advance of the *inkotanyi*. We had in mind sweeping massacres that would chase them away into Burundi and the neighboring countries for good. Nothing more serious than that.

As for the farmers, they heard rumors here and there; they welcomed the prospect of freeing up new fields, but they were most concerned with their own crops. They got all fired up the morning after the plane crash, not before. But afterward they had no problem understanding that this time it was for good.

IGNACE: The authorities had made lists of the important Tutsis in the commune—teachers and shopkeepers, for example. We already knew these people had to be killed first, though their families would be left alone. We were not to bother with the farmers and Tutsis of lesser interest. But after listing the influential people, the authorities announced the families should die, too, and all their neighbors as well. These detailed killings took us by surprise, if I may say so.

JEAN-BAPTISTE: When Habyarimana's republic was forced to become a multiparty state, all the different Hutu parties recruited militias, at first to protect themselves from one another, because things were really hot among the Hutu extremists, and then to focus on the Tutsis.

The *interahamwe* were the most visible: they sang in the meetings, paraded in the streets, got together for exercise workouts at the cultural center. They received food, drinks, and little gifts of money from shopkeepers.

They were preparing for small massacres of Tutsis, the way we had been doing them since 1959—punishment massacres, caused by envy, or the *inkotanyi*, or revenge, or greed for Tutsi cows and plots of land. But the removal of all Tutsis—that they thought of only after the plane crash.

Through my job as the municipal census taker, I was well acquainted with the councilor in Ntarama, and I know he did not use the word *genocide* before it began, not even in his innermost thoughts. The higher-ups in Kigali had planned it all behind blank faces.

Innocent: "In Kibungo, we had a very nice councilor named Servilien Kambali, a rich farmer who never wanted any problems on his hill. During the ethnic massacres of 1992, he had behaved quite calmly and had separated groups of troublemakers without even a single dead man on either side. He was a Hutu, of a peaceful disposition.

"On April 10, three days after the crash, he warned his people: 'All right, it is too hot in the country—but I will not accept commotion or bloodshed in my sector. I am setting out for Nyamata to bring back security reinforcements. Until I return, do not leave your houses, all of you, or it will go badly with you. Anyone who utters a threat will be punished. Anyone who lifts a hand, watch out.'

"In Nyamata he explained about the hotheads and asked for

help. The burgomaster replied, 'Servilien, you're an idiot. No more of your screw-ups. Instead of reinforcements, you will return to your hill with strict orders.'

"When Servilien came back, he told the Hutu farmers waiting for him in a circle: 'Well, it's already been decided. They have already started. We must kill them all.' He grabbed a gun, and from then on he was out in front as a prominent organizer, from the first day to the last.

"Could that fellow remain a nice guy in the middle of the genocide? Obviously not, if he wanted to keep his position as councilor. And if he wanted his share of the spoils, he clearly couldn't sit on his front porch with his arms crossed. Since he was well known, he couldn't lie low on his hill watching it all, either, without risking the wrath of the Hutu youths.

"But he could certainly have behaved timidly in killing and seeking advantages. He could have lagged behind the advancing line, or gone to Gitarama with his family, if it disgusted him to get out his gun. At his trial, he said it had never occurred to him."

FULGENCE: While a number of educated people were organizers, others were simple killers, same as the farmers; they worked as we did, without seeming any smarter at the killings. Some of them hid their ambitions; others revealed them. It depended on the authority they wanted to acquire later on, after everything was taken care of. It depended on their future aspirations. All in all, they didn't behave any worse than we did.

PIO: Some educated people, shopkeepers and so on, spoke with such ferocity that the least the authorities could do was repay their enthusiasm by lending them guns, so they wouldn't get their clothes bloodied. They shot, they shouted, they toed the line:

they lined up with the leaders for words and with the followers for actions. The killings by these intimidators were more conventional and less messy than ours.

LÉOPORD: The organizers arranged patrols, settled disputes over looting, and laid out the daily itineraries. If these organizers hadn't shown up, it wouldn't have occurred to the farmers to begin the work. They would have brandished machetes in anger over the plane crash and then gone back to their fields. Or let's say they would have sweated it out in the marshes, but not for so many days. They would have bided their time. That all-out decision to kill, that was definitely from the organizers.

ADALBERT: The educated people were certainly the ones who drove the farmers on, out in the marshes. Today they're the ones who juggle with words or turn close-mouthed. Many sit quietly in their same places as before. Some have become ministers or bishops; they aren't so much in the public eye, but they still wear their fancy clothes and gold-framed glasses. While suffering keeps us in prison.

IGNACE: The organizers could always leave if they didn't feel all right about the daily killings. They could sit around discussing schedules or go visit distant relatives—unlike the farmers, who didn't know how to fend for themselves in town. But the organizers did all stay. Those who didn't step into the front ranks got along fine at the back. They wanted to make sure they were noticed, or to make sure they got theirs.

BEHIND THE *MUDUGUDUS*

The first *mudugudus* sprang up shortly after the genocide and spread throughout Rwanda, appearing mainly near hilltop villages and occasionally along paths or near small streams in the bush. In Kibungo you can see a *mudugudu* by turning off a bush trail just before you reach the first houses; there is another in Kanzenze on an unpaved road that climbs up from the taxi-bus stop, and another in a clearing downhill from the church in Ntarama.

This pretty word does not mean anything particularly pretty. A *mudugudu* is a cluster of standard-issue houses, a clump of lined-up rectangles. The most impressive settlements contain three thousand units, the more modest ones about thirty. Depending on where they are and who paid for them, the houses are built of fired brick, concrete, or adobe, with or without window frames, and roofed, of course, in corrugated metal.

Nicolae Ceaușescu's conception of a Rumanian village, the Israeli kibbutz, and the Soviet *kolkhoz* (minus Soviet collectivism) were all models for the *mudugudu* project. This rearrangement of rural living conditions served two purposes: it provided emergency housing to replace the countless homes, mostly Tutsi, destroyed during the war, and it offered better security for peasant families who had once lived scattered throughout the jungle and the bush.

This type of urban consolidation and the resulting abandonment of isolated little villages is distressing, at first glance, to a

Westerner familiar with previous catastrophic experiments. Most of the Rwandans who live in *mudugudus* do not share such reservations, however. Francine Niyitegeka, Berthe Mwanankabandi, Claudine Kayitesi, Angélique Mukamanzi, and Christine Nyiransabimana, whom I wrote about in my book on the Tutsi survivors, all abandoned their family homes, which they could neither rebuild nor repair, and moved into *mudugudus* with their children. The women say they feel safer and are much better off there, in spite of the unfamiliar crowding, the several kilometers now separating them from their plots of land, the loss of walled farmyards and flower and kitchen gardens, and the absence of the scarlet-black-and-yellow *gonoleks*, the long-tailed little *souimanga* sunbirds, and Rwanda's marvelous nightingales.

To understand this withdrawal, we should think about these words from Francine: "When you have experienced a waking nightmare in real life, you no longer sort through your daytime and nighttime thoughts the way you did before. Ever since the genocide, I always feel hunted, night and day. In my bed, I turn away from shadows; on a path, I look back at forms following me. I fear for my child when I meet a stranger's eyes. Sometimes I see the face of an *interahamwe* near the river and tell myself, Look, Francine, you've seen that man before in a dream, and I remember only afterward that the dream was in real time, wide awake, back then in the marshes."

Less obtrusive than the *mudugudus*, other features appear or reappear, to the surprise of strangers and native Rwandans alike. In Nyamata new churches are going up beside the old ones, all of them packed during services, especially the funerals attended every week by hundreds or thousands of the faithful. The trumpeting muezzin of a mosque frequented by repatriates from Uganda startles the village awake twice a night. A slew of local and international Christian sects flourishes even to the farthest reaches of the bush.

In Nyamata the commune has become a district, and the burgomaster a mayor. Here and there computers with the promise of e-mail and the Internet await a telephone jack or the return to work of an ailing engineer. The cultural center, once occupied by the militias under Joseph-Désiré Bitero's command, now hosts a reading club in the morning and television shows in the afternoon. At night dozens of recently acquired TVs join antediluvian radios in a vain attempt to overpower the mooing, croaking, clicking, and cooing of cows, frogs, crickets, and turtledoves.

On Sundays the Bugesera Sport soccer team, renamed Nyamata FC, shows off the more fashionable red and white jerseys that replaced its old purple ones, and although the team has not yet regained its former brio, exuberant fans, or commercial sponsors, it proves its optimism with practice sessions three times a week.

On Wednesdays and Saturdays the market is vibrant with the swirling colors of the vendors' clothes, the fabrics piled on the ground, and the umbrellas deployed against the glare. This is the only place where the air hums with hope for a bright future. On market days, farm women, women wholesalers and retailers, fishermen's wives, stockmen, craftsmen—all find themselves back again, side by side, delivering their usual patter, while the hill people stream in at dawn for a day in Nyamata. The square smells just like old times, traffic jams return to the main street, and the *cabarets* are noisy once again. Jostling throngs visit the mills, the veterinary and medical clinics, the slaughterhouse, the post office, and the town hall.

Hutu and Tutsi families crowd the church pews to pray, their eyes on the priests; perched on their school benches, kids listen to their teachers; at the soccer field, people cheer or boo the teams, but the market is the only place where they speak normally to one another, haggling and joking. As Rose Kubwimana, Adalbert's mother, says, "At the market Hutus recover the spirit to be themselves as they were before." It's a kind of pleasant interlude, before people return to the isolation of their neighborhoods or hills.

Up on the hills, the coffee plantations, which need three or four years of care to become productive again, still lie fallow, but the banana groves already show pale green against the darker vegetation of the countryside. More people are drinking more *urwagwa* than ever before, although quality may not have kept pace with quantity.

In Kibungo there are already two *cabarets*: Francine's is patronized exclusively by survivors, while the one across the way caters to a more "mixed" clientele, as they say here. On the central square Hutu and Tutsi women strip beans by slapping the plants against jute sacks. A tailor has set up a Singer sewing machine. A diesel-powered mill now spares farm women a trek of twenty kilometers lugging sacks on their backs to grind their harvests of sorghum and manioc. Hundreds of kids dribble a foam-rubber ball around the schoolyard, and cows take advantage of abandoned houses to calve in comfort.

At the bottom of the road leading down the other slope of Kibungo, pirogues glide along the stagnant river through reeds and water lilies in the company of pelicans, sacred ibises, and white flamingos, which have all been irreproachably faithful to these waters. The fishermen are still Hutus, and they dry-smoke their black fish—which they never eat themselves—over live charcoal before stringing them onto vines. The cattlemen of the surrounding area are still Tutsis, who neither milk nor eat their

Ankole cows. The prime showcase for these powerful horned beasts and their owners, who carry staffs and wear their traditional felt slouch hats, had once been the *igiterane*, the Tuesday stock fair, but it has yet to return to the clearing in Kayumba; negotiations are currently conducted in private. The community has restored its cattle holdings to their prewar numbers, however, and the animals roam the bush even more freely, in groups watched over once again by cowherds dressed in the rags believed to protect their charges from envious eyes.

The major innovation is the erection of hedges of prickly euphorbia along paths to protect field crops. Ten years earlier such barriers were a sacrilege, and the dispute over them was reminiscent of the nineteenth-century range wars between farmers and cattlemen on the prairies of the American West, but today they no longer provoke outrage.

Years have passed since the genocide. Now that the refugees have returned to these Hutu and Tutsi communities, forced by fate to live together despite the genocide, the constant question is—how are they getting along? There are promising signs in Nyamata: noisy, happy wedding celebrations on Saturday afternoons, the construction of an antenna for cell phones, a brand-new hospital, the departure of the humanitarian organizations, the fashion for black, pink, and almond-green seats in the pedicabs, the reaccreditation of examinations at the Lycée Apebu, the rivalry between two hardware stores over the sale of corrugated metal sheets, the appearance of the first new detached houses . . .

Another answer is that the fear is still there, ever present, and there is no way of knowing how many generations it will torment before it fades away.

It is the fear experienced by Angélique: "I saw many people

cut down beside me, and all this time I have battled a tenacious fear, truly overwhelming terror. I have overcome it, but I cannot say it has let go of me for good."

Or the fear felt by Hutu children, as Sylvie described it: "For the Hutu youngsters who went to Congo, the oppression remains, because they are not facing the past. Silence is paralyzing them with fright. Time is holding them back. From visit to visit, I find no change. One can see that anxiety is stifling their thoughts. It is such hard work to encourage them to speak, but they can never set foot back in life if they don't talk about what they must confront within themselves."

On the path down the slope where the families of Pio, Pancrace, and Adalbert live is the house of Denise Nikuze, a twenty-year-old Hutu woman. Magnificent flowers bloom within the dilapidated walls of her courtyard. Together Denise and her sister, Jacqueline Dusabimana, are raising their children born of "love on the run, affairs that bring small advantages."

In a faded T-shirt and skirt, Denise goes to her field at dawn. Wrapping her infant in a cloth, she places it in the shelter of an avocado tree and plies her hoe until midafternoon without anything to eat or drink. On Sundays she wears her lace-trimmed dress to church in Kibungo, occasionally walking a few hundred meters farther to the shops to buy soap or oil, but sometimes she prefers to walk the twenty-five kilometers to Nyamata, where she doesn't feel so many eyes upon her.

Denise Nikuze is very sweet, hospitable, and intelligent. She offers us *urwagwa* and some pineapple from the marshes. At the mention of the killings she falls silent, except to say, "Terrible sickness came for my mother during that bad time. Death carried off papa amid a mystery of rumors. My three brothers were scattered during the confusions, perhaps to Congo, perhaps to a prison far away . . . somewhere I may never know about. Here I meet only passing lovers who will never hold me with the arms of a real husband. No one threatens me anymore, but I hear no words of conciliation, either. From now on I see only silence to protect me from fear and the evil shadows that stalk our fields."

Farther along the road, we meet Rose and Pancrace's sister, Marthe, sitting on their doorsteps shelling beans or grinding sorghum. They are gracious, sometimes funny, as well as curious about a world they have vaguely heard about on the radio; they are eager for news from Rilima, but without turning hostile, they fall silent whenever mention is made of the bloodstained past.

LIFE GOES ON

ALPHONSE: In the evenings old folks would ask quietly, "Why don't we simply kill the trampling cows, take some prime fields, and still leave plenty of Tutsis alive?" The leader would reply, "No. Their tradition is too ancient. Tutsis have been trailing after their cattle for too long, they will start over again with new cows. Slaughtering cows and Tutsis, it's the same task."

When I get out of prison, I don't know if I will learn to see cows in a favorable light. Hutus are not used to cows; encountering herds by the water or in the bush makes them uneasy. But as for the damage from their hoofs, we will work things out better than before, with the help of polite compensations like a sack of seed grain or a case of Primus. And we'll put up euphorbia hedges around the planting fields. Slaughter and vengeance—for me, that is really over.

ÉLIE: In the camps many came to feel intimidated by what they had done, and others changed in prison, like me. I wrote short notes of apology to some families of victims I knew and had them delivered by visitors. I denounced myself and I spoke of my guilt to the families of people I killed. When I get out, I will take gifts, food and drink; I will offer enough Primus beer and brochettes for proper reconciliation gatherings.

After that, I'm going to take up ordinary life again, but this time with a good will. I'm going to turn a kind eye on my neighbors bright and early every morning. I want to sow my plot of land, or weld, or saw wood, or do masonry; I'll eagerly accept odd jobs. Or be a soldier if necessary in patriotic and dangerous situations, except without aiming or shooting a gun. From now on, I don't want to kill even a highway robber anymore.

PIO: I think that if Providence helps me get out of prison, I won't waste my days as I do now. I'll go back to my hill and look for a good wife; because of the events, I am still a single man. I see nothing to keep me from a proper life. Anyway, I find no satisfaction in going somewhere else so as to hide from angry looks. A stained life is better than one that isn't mine anymore.

If forgetting is merciful, I shall be grateful. If the opportunity arises, I shall express my regrets; if the opportunity returns, I shall apologize again. I shall make patience and shyness my companions. I am truly finished with playing the tough guy. If life in good company was possible before, it still ought to be, in spite of those stupid killings.

In any case, we must all get used to the evil we experienced, even if this wickedness took different forms for different people. Because we all had to bear it in our own way.

JOSEPH-DÉSIRÉ: Since I am condemned to die, I am condemned to grab hold of this life shadowed by sudden and unnatural death. In our courtyard, sixty of us are forced by fate to wait, to play *igisoro*, to keep an ear turned to what the outside world is saying, thanks to the radio. It is a different life from the one I used to lead, not at all like the one I chose. But it is still a life, which is mine, and if I do not take it, no one will offer me another.

FULGENCE: I believe the consequences have been most unfortunate for us all. The others have gathered in many dead. But we, too, have met with perilous hardships in the camps and a wretched life in prison. In exile, sickness robbed me of two children, my mother, some compatriots, and I am suffering from this imprisonment.

Time has punished me for my misdeeds and can allow me to begin an ordinary life again when I leave here. After those killings and those ordeals, I no longer see Evil the way I used to: I am going to become a more normal person.

I don't know how my neighbors will receive me, because I haven't had a chance to speak with them. I think I will manage to convince them to live beside us as before, at least in appearance. I feel a great longing for the living, I am impatient to be among them.

PANCRACE: From now on, a huge wasteland separates the living and the dead. But the living must carry on in this world. Back on my hill, I am going to ask my neighbors to live once more in harmony. I will ask time to help me look for a good wife and find ways to make do with my plot of land. When work begins again in the fields, I will propose mutual assistance to the Tutsi neighbors. I don't know if they will accept it as before, but I will offer it without restrictions to show my honest intentions.

Aside from the anguish of my years in prison, I do not see my life as harmed by all these regrettable events. Fortune and misfortune have not changed me. As for the others, it's not for me to say; the matter is too delicate.

JEAN-BAPTISTE: I feel more at peace since I began to speak. After I have endured my punishment, I see nothing to prevent me from returning to my wife, my place in society, my six children, even if they have grown up without me and no longer recognize me. I must point out something, however: there is now a crack in my life. I don't know about the others. I don't know if it's because of my Tutsi wife. But I do know that the clemency of justice or the compassion of the stricken families can never fix this crack. Even the resurrection of the victims might not fix it. Perhaps not even my death will fix it.

IGNACE: I am a good farmer, and I no longer own even one basic tool. My children have scattered far and wide without sending me comforting words. I receive no news about the soundness of my house. I haven't walked upon my hill since the killings. I am discouraged. Sometimes I feel terrified by the look in the eyes of the survivors who wait for me. I feel disappointed by all I have lost.

When I get out, I think I will manage for food. But comfort and respect, as before—I can tell already these are gone for good. My life zigzags in prison, always banging into things, and the only goal I can find for it is my field back home. I yearn to hold the hoe firmly in my own two hands, to bend to my work without hearing another word, except talk about crops.

FULGENCE: What we did goes beyond human imagination, so it is too difficult to judge us—too difficult for those who did not share our situation, in any case. Therefore I think we must be farmers like before, this time with good thoughts; we must show our regrets at all times; we must give a little something to those who have suffered. And leave to God the too-heavy task of our final punishment.

LÉOPORD: Someone who is touched by repentance for the blood he has shed, good fortune can take that person in hand, and he can start over again on his hill like before. Same for someone willing to speak without fear of being punished more, someone who tells the neighbors what he did with his machete.

But if he keeps saying he remembers nothing or only piddling things—that he wasn't there and suchlike nonsense—if he bows down to lies in the hope of evading retribution and reproach, then he will be driven even farther from his home. There are many such liars.

In prison, most killers consider their failure the most important reason for their present misery. Same thing on the hills. They say they have come too far without the Tutsis to turn around now. They think they will never again find a worthwhile place alongside the Tutsis they did not completely weed out. They say they will be the rejects in the present situation.

They stew too much in vengeance to have any hope of hauling themselves out, looking around at the new developments on their hills, and accepting a normal life under the Tutsis' watchful eye. They will always be spitters of wicked words.

ADALBERT: Back in Kibungo I will tend to my fields and my family. The killings and prison have aged me, they have tempered me. I don't feel so hot-headed anymore. I've lost my taste for revelry and commotion.

With the survivors, I do not know what will happen. There are people in Kibungo who will be able to understand me, but only those who plied their machetes like me or more than me. The Tutsis, though—it's unthinkable for them to learn and understand. You just can't ask them to see our actions as we did. I believe their suffering will reject any kind of explanation. What we have done is unnatural to them. Perhaps patience and forgetting will win out; perhaps not.

BARGAINING FOR FORGIVENESS

Must one forgive? What good is forgiveness? Does it help reveal the truth? ease the mourning of survivors? encourage the healing reconciliation vital to future generations?

Who can forgive? Can one forgive in the name of someone else, a relative, a friend, particularly if that person has disappeared? Can one forgive someone who does not ask to be forgiven, or who makes no sincere effort to be forgiven, or who refuses forgiveness? Are there several ways to forgive? different degrees or stages of forgiveness? If one feels unable to forgive, can one ask another—God or someone more humane—to forgive in one's place? What commitment is made by the one seeking forgiveness? by the one granting it? Such questions are as old as humanity.

In *Memory, History, Forgetting*, the philosopher Paul Ricoeur writes, "Can one forgive someone who does not admit his guilt? Must the person forgiving the offender have been offended against? Can one forgive oneself? Even if an author comes down on one side or the other of these questions (and how could he not, at least if the philosopher's job entails more than simply describing dilemmas), there will always be room for objections."

For half a century, contemporary conflicts that purposefully target civilian populations have posed new questions about forgiveness. Can one grant it to the authors of collective crimes? of state crimes, or crimes against humanity? Can one grant collective pardon to a community that actively participated in or passively condoned such crimes, to a people united in their support for them, to a state guilty of crimes on a massive scale? to those who seek forgiveness but take no responsibility for their crimes?

Can you forgive, in the aftermath of a genocide, those who tried to exterminate you?

Several years after the events, the Bugesera survivors are almost unanimous in replying no to that last question, although they cannot say whether their position might evolve over time. To understand this refusal, consider the replies of three survivors of the Nyamata marshes who can speak for their companions.

First, Francine, a farm woman and shopkeeper in Kibungo who was a neighbor of the gang members: "Sometimes, when I sit alone in a chair on my veranda, I imagine this possibility: one far-off day, a local man comes slowly up to me and says, 'Bonjour, Francine. I have come to speak to you. So, I am the one who cut your mama and your little sisters. I want to ask your forgiveness.' Well, to that person I cannot reply anything good. A man may ask for forgiveness if he has had one Primus too many and then beats his wife. But if he has worked at killing for a whole month, even on Sundays, whatever can he hope to be forgiven for?

"We must simply go back to living, since life has so decided . . . We shall return to drawing water together, to exchanging neighborly words, to selling grain to one another. In twenty years, fifty years, there will perhaps be boys and girls who will learn about the genocide in books. For us, though, it is impossible to forgive."

Now Sylvie, a social worker out on the hills and a baker in the town of Nyamata: "In the deepest part of me, it is a question not of forgiving or forgetting but of reconciling. The white who let the killers work, there is nothing to forgive him for. The Hutu who massacred, there is nothing to forgive him for. Someone who watched a neighbor open the bellies of girls to kill the babies before their mamas' eyes, there is nothing to forgive. There's no point in wasting words talking to him about it. Only justice can pardon . . . a justice that makes room for truth, so that fear will drain away . . .

"One day, perhaps, living together or helping one another will come back among the families of those who killed and those who were killed. But for us, it is too late, because from now on there will be a void. We stepped forward into life, we were cut, and we retreated. It is too heartbreaking, for human beings, to find themselves fallen behind where they once were in life."

Finally, Édith, a school bursar and a Catholic proselyte who goes from church to church in the hills. She is the only one of these three women to envisage the possibility of forgiveness, which she understands, however, as a kind of mystic absolution: "I know that all the Hutus who killed so calmly cannot be sincere when they beg pardon, even of the Lord. But me, I am ready to forgive. It is not a denial of the harm they did, not a betrayal of the Tutsis, not an easy way out. It is so that I will not suffer my whole life long asking myself why they tried to cut me. I do not want to live in remorse and fear from being Tutsi. If I do not forgive them, it is I alone who suffers and frets and cannot sleep . . . I yearn for peace in my body. I really must find tranquillity. I have to sweep fear far away from me, even if I do not believe their soothing words."

We can see, then, that the survivors and the killers do not show the same understanding of forgiveness or pardon, and that itself may make forgiveness impossible.

Of all the active and passive protagonists in the Rwandan genocide—survivors, killers, repatriates, witnesses from political, religious, and humanitarian organizations—the survivors are the least preoccupied with forgiveness. Even though they are distressed by the prospect of reconciliation, they will speak of it only when asked.

The killers, on the contrary, mention forgiveness the most often, but with a disconcerting naïveté, as the following pages will show. The killers' and survivors' differing ideas of forgiveness illustrate two distinct visions of the future and of their changed relationship.

Speaking of which, I should note a new and essential distinction between ordinary war criminals and the perpetrators of genocide. The former, while equally guilty of savagery when they destroy, torture, and rape, often prove able, with time, to reflect on the effort and grace demanded by forgiveness—from both their victims and themselves. But the killers of the Kibungo gang, while they speak frequently of forgiveness, and hope to receive it, do not use the questioning language of self-examination. The way they see it, pardon—whether collective or individual, useful or useless, painful or not—comes on its own and is available upon request.

Strangely, the prisoners can imagine what resentment, anger, and distrust mean to a survivor, they can understand the spirit or act of revenge, and they accept the plausibility of these violent responses to their return. But they simply cannot fathom what the act of forgiveness would mean to a survivor. Some prisoners see it as an obligatory first step; for others, it is a mysterious gesture that will depend on the kindness or the personality of the interlocutor. But either way it boils down to a renunciation of revenge.

It can also be a sort of bargain, a trade-off—so many confessions for so much forgiveness—or a formality. Since I have been punished, I have been pardoned, because the hardship of my sentence brings proportionate forgiveness. Or forgiveness vaguely represents an opportunity: forgiving is forgetting, the best way for everyone to return to the good old days and start over as if nothing had ever happened. The killer seems oblivious to the minimum requirement for those seeking forgiveness: that they tell the truth, with no tactical calculations, in order to help the victims in their work of remembrance and mourning.

The killer has no idea of the ordeal that begins for the victims once they have agreed to forgive, for in so doing they not only reopen old wounds but also lose the possibility of gaining relief through revenge. The killer does not understand that in seeking forgiveness, he is demanding that the victim make an extraordinary effort, and he remains oblivious to the survivor's dilemma, anguish, and courageous altruism. The killer does not realize that when he asks for forgiveness as though it were a simple formality, his attitude increases the victim's pain by ignoring it.

The killer does not grasp that truth, sincerity, and forgiveness are bound together. For him, more or less telling the truth is a recommended ploy for more or less diminishing his offense and, thus, his punishment, even his guilt. Asking for pardon is thus a selfish act invested in the future, because it facilitates his reunion with family and friends, promotes his rehabilitation, and helps him renew former relationships.

In the preceding chapter, Élie said, "I wrote short notes of apology to some families of victims I knew and had them delivered by visitors." The killers make their requests for forgiveness in writing, or from the witness stand, or via common acquaintances. During our visits to Rilima, Innocent is earnestly importuned several times in this way by prisoners hoping he will seek forgiveness in their name from survivors in Kibungo.

Élie and most of the others in the gang do not ask for forgiveness. They offer their apologies in more or less loud voices to survivors who are free to hear, accept, or refuse them—rather like the way one says "Sorry" to somebody one has just jostled on a sidewalk. Or like that German soldier in the strange parable told by Simon Wiesenthal in *The Sunflower*, they ask for pardon with the certainty that this request, because it is humiliating and expresses sympathy, deserves in itself a positive response.

These observations bring to mind others the reader has probably made while considering the killers' comments on their memories and dreams. The killers insist that the dreams reflect mainly their former lives: family, work in the fields, the countryside, *cabarets*. This is understandable if one recalls how quickly they abandoned that domestic universe, carried away by the madness of the massacres before their headlong flight into exile. The description of their nightmares, however, is more perplexing.

Most of them claim not to have nightmares—unlike their victims, who are tormented at night by haunting, distressing, appalling dreams from which they awaken in an agony of guilt. And when the killers do have their rare nightmares, these are about the horrors of prison or the camps in Congo rather than the killing season in the marshes.

Is this possible? Is it possible that of all categories of war criminals, the perpetrator of genocide winds up the least traumatized? Is it believable that sleep would so thoroughly mask such extraordinary acts and feelings? Are their victims truly so absent from their nightmares? If so, how do they elude the pangs of remorse in their dreams without the protection of lies? To what do they owe the indulgence of their unconscious minds, their bizarre ability to bolt the gates of slumber against their guilt?

And if this is *not* possible, why do they deny or downplay their nightmares—which they might offer as tangible proof of their repentance and, in a way, some slight repayment of their debt—especially when at the same time, in broad daylight, they tell us of their crimes in great detail? Do they fear being over-whelmed by their descriptions of these dreams, which might contradict or transform their narrative accounts, discredit them, or make them more heinous? Are they afraid that recounting these nightmares might reveal things they wish to keep hidden? Is their silence a way of anticipating their rehabilitation? or simply a refusal to take a backward look, eyes wide open, for fear of what they might see about themselves?

Is there some connection between this reluctance to discuss their nightmares and their incomprehension of forgiveness? Is this a way to dam up their memories, to avoid any risk of losing con-trol of their confessions? to survive, psychologically, what they did?

PARDONS

ÉLIE: The killings were out of our hands, and so is forgiveness. We never properly discussed the killings at the time of the marshes; I do not know if we can talk adequately about forgiveness now that everything is over and done with.

Here is what I say: anyone who let his remorse be glimpsed before the cutting ended and who left the marshes of his own free will, abandoning the job unfinished, or anyone who in that way lost the benefits of looting and the respect of his colleagues—that person could be wholeheartedly forgiven.

But as for the rest of us, what we are offering is prison repentance, so they will give us a pardon of convenience in exchange. It is a pardon, in spite of everything, but the last one on the shelf. A leftover pardon, so to speak. It might turn out to be insignificant if the situation shifts; it might not hold up in the future, under threat of new bloody upheavals.

FULGENCE: To forgive is to erase the offense someone else committed against you.

But you cannot forgive unless you hear a great truth spoken without twisting and turning. Me, I begged pardon of the stricken families during the trial, and I told them of the evil I had done to them. So I think I shall be forgiven. If not, it can't be helped; I will pray.

Forgiveness is a great good fortune: it can ease punishment, relieve remorse, and make forgetting easier. It is a winner for the person who receives it. For the person who gives it, I can't say, because the opportunity has never presented itself to me. I believe that for the person who forgives, it depends on if he is thanked with a suitable compensation.

ADALBERT: Begging pardon is first of all speaking a valid truth to people who have suffered. Secondly, asking them to forget the harm you have done to them or their families. Thirdly, offering to think of them as you did before, without hidden reservations.

If a person agrees at the first try, this is lucky. If not, try again. You should not be discouraged after all the troubles you have already endured. The more steps you take to seek forgiveness, the more often you will see a chance for forgiveness, and the faster you will catch up with it. Especially if the authorities support a program encouraging the survivors to forgive.

JEAN-BAPTISTE: In prison most inmates reject forgiveness. They say, "I apologized and I am still in prison. So what use is it, besides pleasing the authorities?" Or else they keep saying, "Look at that man. He asked forgiveness of everyone at his trial, and he still got a heavy sentence. Forgiveness, for us, from now on it's a waste of time." That is why they prefer to stand fast on their old opinions.

But I am very concerned with forgiveness. And I am certain of being forgiven, because I confessed, because I am convinced of my offense and determined to live in the right way, like before. If someone who has suffered cannot forgive me at first, time will help this person manage it on a better occasion. Forgiveness will help us to forget together, even though in both camps each person may hide away memories of deepest pain and sorrow.

IGNACE: Forgiveness is the grace of God that allows someone who has been pursued and struck to forget. Someone who has lost his wife, his children, his house with all his belongings, his herd, someone who entrusts his grief to God—forgiveness will allow this man to go beyond what he has lived and lost in misfortune.

If the survivor is touched by faith, that is mercy; if not, it is mischance. I know that in the opposite situation, I would manage to forgive my offender, because through thick and thin I have always preserved a great faith in God.

ADALBERT: If I am pardoned by the authorities, if I am pardoned by God, I will be pardoned by my neighbors. It will take time, and the effort will be hard, but this forgiveness is necessary. Without forgiveness, terrible killings might start up again. This forgiveness is a decision of the new policy from the authorities in Kigali. It is too burdensome for neighbors who have suffered to oppose the justice of religion and their country.

PANCRACE: Speaking the truth to someone who has suffered is risky but not wounding. Hearing the truth from a killer is wounding but not risky. Both have their advantage and their disadvantage. So seeking forgiveness is as wrenching as granting it.

Therefore many prisoners prefer begging pardon from God rather than from their neighbors, and they push their way to the front during prayers and hymn-singing. They entrust their forgiveness to God and nothing to their neighbors. With God, words are less dangerous for the future, and more comforting.

ALPHONSE: Forgiveness—that is the favor granted by the person who has suffered the crimes. If the victim hears a proper truth from the offender, a sincere request, he can decide if he wants to forget. If I am pardoned by the authorities and leave prison after my sentence is up, I could tell even more of the truth on my hill than I did at the trial. I will be able to add confessions and memories that I saved in secret for my neighbors. If I am free, I will be able to give details and accounts of the situation in the marshes. I will be able to visit houses and tell what happened to this one and that, to satisfy my listeners' personal need to know and to receive their forgiveness.

But if I am too harshly penalized and must stay in prison too long, I will continue to live here as a killer, without forgiveness, or courage, or truth—in other words, like someone who has lost everything, and not just materially.

IGNACE: I say, if I am suitably pardoned, I will recover a normal frame of mind, my outlook from before; if I am not pardoned, I will keep the attitude of an offender. But it is not me who can speak the words of good intention, it is the survivors. That is why I am impatient. Forgiveness is always very advantageous for whoever receives it.

JOSEPH-DÉSIRÉ: What I did was more seen by others, because I was higher up. It is not a worse offense, but a more visible offense that caused the rejection of my pardon.

LÉOPORD: In the marshes, many Tutsis begged to be spared before the fatal stroke of the machete. They pleaded for mercy, for pity; they asked to escape death or the dreadful agony of the blows. Terror and suffering inspired their words.

They gave all their supplication, because they had nothing else to give. But we could not have cared less about whatever they were asking or even begging for. On the contrary, that could spur us on. They were only Tutsis good for killing, and we were men without pity.

Therefore it is awkward to speak of forgiveness in prison. Outside, if I receive a tornado of fury instead of forgiveness, I will not show any spite. I will take my trouble patiently. I will simply tell people, All right: forgiveness, now it belongs to you, it's on your side, you have certainly earned it. So from now on you can handle it however you like. Me, I can wait for your right moment. I will pick up my life again where it left off without whispering against you.

ÉLIE: There are some people who envy those who didn't have to seek forgiveness, and who returned to their land without crossing the threshold of Rilima. Some people say that those who asked forgiveness have not been properly rewarded and are still in prison; they claim that pardon, for the prisoner, is a hazardous and useless expense.

PIO: Seeking forgiveness is a natural thing. Bestowing forgiveness is a huge thing. But who today can decide this forgiveness? those who did nothing, like the whites and such? those who arrived too late, behind the soldiers of the RPF, coming home with their savings and their memories of revenge? those who happened to elude death by sneaking into the papyrus? Even the mama of the child who was cut, what can she forgive in the name of her little one, who is no longer here to be questioned?

I see too many difficulties for us to exchange forgiveness on the hills. Too many bad memories will grow again on the fine words, like the bush in the middle of a plantation. Someone who grants you forgiveness on a day of mercy, who can say he won't take it back some other day in anger, because of a drunken squabble?

I can't imagine any forgiveness capable of drying up all this spilled blood. I see only God to forgive me—it's why I ask that of Him every day. Offering Him all my sincerity, without hiding any of my misdeeds from Him. I don't know if He says yes or no, but I do know that I ask Him very personally.

A NOBLE BEARING

I have often mentioned the Jewish genocide, and not the Armenian, Gypsy, or Cambodian genocides, because I am more familiar with it—thanks to many memoirs, books, and the film *Shoah*—and because during my visits to Rwanda, I noticed many analogies between the Jewish and Tutsi genocides, especially regarding the way in which they were implemented.

So let's consider a question often raised more or less openly: are the Tutsis, so to speak, the Jews of central Africa's Great Lakes region, of Rwanda in particular? Are they distant cousins of the Jews of Ethiopia, the Falashas, lost on a detour from their destination? Do the fates of the Jews and Tutsis have something in common?

The immediate answer is, obviously not: Jews and Tutsis do not share the same history at all. And yet . . .

Tutsis practice no distinctive religion, do not trace their roots back through any founding holy scripture, and do not speak their own language or dialect. No custom or principle, aside from their traditional cattle breeding, distinguishes their way of life from that of their compatriots. What's more, unlike European Jews, Tutsis have wielded absolute power in Rwanda. In fact, they founded a monarchy that lasted for almost eight centuries, a complex and sophisticated monarchy that left an incisive mark on the collective Hutu memory, although it remains an enigma to historians even today. And yet . . .

One is struck by the similarities not between Jewish and Tutsi mythologies or ways of life but between the expression of European anti-Semitism before the Jewish genocide and the expression of anti-Tutsi feeling before the Rwandan genocide. The elements of anti-Tutsi propaganda are strangely similar to those of anti-Semitic propaganda—in singling out physical characteristics (low or high foreheads, hooked or straight noses, crooked or slender fingers); psychological qualifiers relating to cowardice, slyness, and treachery; and allusions to greed and arrogance. Equivalent terms sum up this correspondence: parasites and cockroaches.

Being neither an ethnologist nor an expert on Africa, I will not weigh in on current discussions of ethnicity (the origin of the concept, its special nature in Africa, its manipulation by colonialists), but as a seasoned traveler, I will make this one remark: in black Africa, people define themselves spontaneously and casually by their ethnic groups. For example: you're drinking with friends at a sidewalk café in Bamako, and after a while you ask one of them, "Who was the girl sitting next to you just now?" The reply will be, "Her? She's a colleague from work. She's really nice, a Sarakole from Kayes." Or you're watching a soccer match in the stadium in Yaoundé and you ask the guy beside you, "Who's number seven, on the Canon team?" He'll answer, "That's so-and-so, a Hausa. He's a touch slow, but he's got a super left foot."

Black Africa is a formidable medley of willingly assumed ethnic identities of a diversity equaled only by the spirit of tolerance that keeps them in equilibrium. And when a seemingly ethnic disturbance breaks out, the conflict is usually in fact chiefly regional (north against south; interior plateau versus the coast), religious (Christians against Muslims), economic (about the appropriation of mines), or social (residential neighborhoods against the business district); the ethnic group is not the true source of violence and misunderstanding but only a mode of defensive assembly. So we must emphasize both the normality in Rwanda of identifying oneself as Hutu or Tutsi and the anomaly, the deviation represented by the anti-Tutsi propaganda during the regime of President Habyarimana.

What was at the bottom of this propaganda? To say colonization would be simplistic. True, Belgium's colonial administration and clergy spent a century working to set Rwanda's—and Burundi's—indigenous ethnic groups against one another (and in their wake came a cohort of anthropologists whose Africanophobic writings stun you with their abject stupidity). But the colonial intelligentsia infested all of Africa in its efforts to stave off the arrival of independence. And although in Rwanda its theories about the native peoples were racist, they were not especially anti-Tutsi.

So then, did Hutus identify Tutsis with Jews, or did Tutsis themselves identify with them—misunderstanding history as certain Serb ideologists tried to do during the war in Yugoslavia, around the theme of a martyred people? A wandering people, a chosen people . . . ? The answer is still no: there was no such identification, at least not on the hills of the Bugesera.

As Jeannette explains, "The history of the Hutus and Tutsis is like the story of Cain and Abel, brothers who no longer understand each other at all because of mere nothings. But I do not believe the Tutsis resemble the Jews, even though both peoples were caught up in genocides. The Tutsis have never been a people chosen to hear the voice of God, the way the Hebrews were in pagan days. The Tutsis are not a people punished for the death of Jesus Christ. The Tutsis are simply a people come to misfortune on the hills because of their noble bearing."

Until the genocide in 1994, country people in Rwanda knew about Jews only what they had learned from the Bible: Noah's ark, the judgment of Solomon, Moses and the flight from Egypt, the parting of the Red Sea, Calvary on the Mount of

Olives—but nothing about Treblinka or the mass emigrations and pogroms leading up to it. So when Jeannette, Claudine, Angélique, Innocent, and the other survivors discovered during our interviews that they were not the first to have lived through the experience of extermination, they were staggered.

Francine clarified what Jeannette meant by "noble bearing": "Hutus still suffer from a bad idea of Tutsis. The truth is, our physiognomy is the root of the problem: our longer muscles, our more delicate features, our proud carriage. That is all I can think of—the imposing appearance that is our birthright."

To which Claudine adds, "Many Hutus could not bear Tutsis anymore, and that's the truth. Why? That stubborn question haunts the banana groves. I can see there are differences between the two groups that make the Hutus resentful. Tutsis sometimes have longer necks and straighter noses. They are more sober of disposition and more affected in their manner . . . But as to wealth and intelligence, there is no difference at all. Many Hutus distrust a so-called malice in the Tutsi character that simply does not exist."

More perplexed, Sylvie wonders, "I have been looking for some clue I cannot find. I know Hutus did not feel at ease with Tutsis. They decided to not see them anymore anywhere, to feel more comfortable among themselves. But why? I have no answer. I do not know if I bear on my face or on my body some special marks they cannot endure. Sometimes I say no, that can't be it— being tall and slender, with delicate, gentle features, all that silliness. Sometimes I say yes, that really is what began to grow deep inside them. It is an utter madness that even those who killed can no longer manage to contemplate, still less those who were supposed to die."

Why this obsession with physical and cultural difference, so incongruous in Africa? Why—in the Rwandan countryside—this repeated theme about the Tutsis' haughty or statuesque bearing, regular features, and malice? One finds nothing like this in, for example, Kenya, Senegal, or Chad, peopled by Masai, Fulani, and Toubou. Is it something left over from the castes and rituals of the reign of the *mwami* kings?

It's impossible to say, which deepens the mystery of the genocide. There is no one convincing explanation of the roots of anti-Tutsi feeling, which are to my mind as disturbing and unintelligible as those of anti-Semitism. Consider Élie's words when he says, "Influenced by time, the atmosphere encouraged me to distrust the Tutsis. Even when I observed them to be kind and gentle, I had to see them as menacing because of shadowy rumors."

In 1992, a fascinating book by the American scholar Christopher Browning was published, *Ordinary Men: Reserve Police Battalion 101 and the Final Solution in Poland*, the history of a battalion sent to the region around Lublin in Poland, where between July 1942 and November 1943 the Germans murdered some 40,000 Jews and deported about 45,000. The author, a Holocaust expert, worked from documents—chiefly transcripts from the interrogations of 210 of the policemen, conducted between 1962 and 1967 by German magistrates—to reconstruct and analyze the experience of the reservists from Hamburg who were caught up in a demented killing machine. In one chapter, Browning wonders about the general reluctance of the police reservists to acknowledge the anti-Semitism driving them at the time. Why should they deny an obvious attitude that pervaded every institution of the Third Reich, influenced the Nazi officials' decisions, and could therefore be construed as an attenuating circumstance in their favor?

Among the author's many hypotheses is this one:

For a member of the battalion, acknowledging his own anti-Semitism meant compromising his chances of emerging unscathed from his interrogation, and bringing up the anti-Semitism of the battalion as a whole meant accusing his comrades . . . This unwillingness to speak of anti-Semitism also stems, however, from an attitude of political denial . . . For the men to admit that their behavior had an explicitly political and ideological dimension, and that the Nazi moral philosophy seemed reasonable to them at the time, means admitting that they were simply political whirligigs, turning docilely with the wind at every change of regime. And that is a truth few among them can or will confront.

The contexts in which the German and Rwandan killers explain themselves are different: the former gave their testimony as free men, more than twenty years after the fact and over an extended period of time, but they were facing prosecutors who could conceivably indict them, and their testimony was filtered through court clerks.

But I mention these passages because the Kibungo gang is also reluctant to admit that anti-Tutsi sentiment affected them in the marshes. After all, someone who claims as Adalbert does—"The Hutu infant was swaddled with hatred for the Tutsis before first opening his eyes to the world"—might well exonerate himself to a certain extent by insisting that he was brainwashed.

And yet, no: they find it much harder to deal with anti-Tutsi sentiment than to talk about their first murder. It takes hours of discussion before they agree to address the subject. Their reticence leads me to wonder about issues like those raised by Browning (whose book I read only after I had been in Rwanda) and about other pragmatic questions.

Do the killers fear that admitting their anti-Tutsi feelings will complicate their return to the hills, reinforcing their neighbors' distrust? These neighbors might think that someone confessing to ingrained anti-Tutsi opinions has no reason to change and thus remains dangerous. But for the killers to fear this would be naïve, even absurd, given that their enthusiastic performance in the marshes, well known to neighbors and survivors, was enough to earn them a chilly reception *ad vitam aeternam*.

Have they discussed—are they discussing—this among themselves? They hardly ever reply. Were they all equally anti-Tutsi? During our conversations it develops that no, they were not, quite the contrary. But paradoxically their differences bolster their unwillingness to speak about this, since bringing them into the open might undermine their solidarity.

Jean-Baptiste, for example, happily married to a Tutsi and living on a hillside inhabited by Tutsi families, harbored no anti-Tutsi feelings at the beginning of the genocide, only all-consuming fear and ambition. Pio, a youth whose passions ran to soccer rather than politics, never cared a whit for anti-Tutsiism, so long as he got the ball in a position to score. Even Joseph-Désiré Bitero, leader of the *interahamwe*, a terrifying criminal if ever there was one, was not rabidly anti-Tutsi until the last few months before the massacres. The cases of Pancrace, Élie, Fulgence, or Adalbert are a little more complicated, but the different attitudes toward Tutsis did not keep any of the gang from sharing equally in the killing.

Other offenders, once released from prison, have said things out in their fields or in *cabarets* that are shockingly anti-Tutsi, on the other hand. This tends to prove that if anti-Tutsiism was a driving force of the genocide, helping to push it into criminal reality, the bigotry was only one motive of many and not sufficient on its own to explain everyone's actions and attitudes. Ignace, for example, one of the most vicious Tutsi-haters and certainly the most outspoken anti-Tutsi in the gang, is one of those who swung his machete the least.

The gang members have a kind of intuition, more perceptible in their silence than in their words, that helps to explain their reluctance to discuss their anti-Tutsi feelings during the genocide. Although they are not disturbed by their killings, they often seem befuddled or overwhelmed by them. They assert that they were carried away in a tumult, an uproar, a commotion—words they often use. They dread facing the consequences of the genocide, and never inquire about what they might be. More important, they are afraid to learn the reasons and motives behind the upheaval and see no point in trying to understand it. They seem intuitively to understand one danger in particular, which Pio outlines this way: "In some years' time, setting foot once more in the marshes, where we left our footprints—that can be possible if we step carefully. But forcing memory back into our innermost thoughts and the disastrous broodings of childhood . . . a mind can lose itself that way. Especially if the soul has gone astray as ours have."

HATRED OF THE TUTSIS

ADALBERT: Basically, Hutus and Tutsis had been playing dirty tricks on one another since 1959. That was the word from our elders. In the evenings, Primus in hand, they called the Tutsis weaklings, too high and mighty. So Hutu children grew up asking no questions, listening hard to all this nastiness about Tutsis.

After 1959 the oldsters jabbered in the *cabarets* about eliminating all the Tutsis and their herds of trampling cows. That came up often around the bottle: it was a familiar concern to them, like the crops or other business matters. We young people made fun of their old-folks grumbling, but we didn't mind it.

All through his youth, a Hutu could certainly choose a Tutsi friend, hang out and drink with him, but he could never trust him. For a Hutu, a Tutsi might always be a deceiver. He would act nice and seem obliging, but underneath he was constantly scheming. He had to be a natural target of suspicion.

JEAN-BAPTISTE: Hutus have always reproached Tutsis for their great height and for trying to use this to rule. Time has never dried up that bitterness. In Nyamata, as I told you, people said that Tutsi women seemed too slender to stay on our hills, that their skin was smooth from their secret drinking of milk, that their fingers were too delicate to grab a hoe, and all that foolishness.

In truth, Hutus noticed none of that hearsay in the Tutsi women of their neighborhood, who bent their backs beside the Hutu wives and lugged water home the same way they did. Yet

Hutus enjoyed repeating such common talk. They would also murmur that a Hutu with a Tutsi wife, like me, was trying to show off.

They took pleasure in spreading the most unlikely rubbish so as to drive a thin wedge of discord between the two ethnic groups. The important thing was to keep a distance between them and try to aggravate the situation. For example, on the first day of school the teacher had to call out the background of every pupil, so that the Tutsis would feel timid about taking their seats in a class of Hutus.

IGNACE: If a Hutu youth wanted to marry a Tutsi girl, his family would refuse to mark off a section of its banana plantation for him to gather his personal harvest and feed his family. If a Tutsi youth wanted to marry a Hutu girl, his family would refuse to cut him out even one or two cows from the herd to begin breeding for the future. That way young people in both camps saw no interest in spending time together.

Hatred flourished in the fields because the plots of land were not large enough for two ethnic groups.

FULGENCE: Actually, Hutus did not detest Tutsis as much as that. Not enough to kill them all, anyway. Evil spells much worse than stubborn hatred meddled in this ethnic rivalry and sent us into those marshes. Lack of land, for example—we spoke seriously about that among ourselves. We could clearly see we would soon run out of fertile fields. We told ourselves that our children would have to leave one by one, seeking land over by Gitarama or farther away, toward Tanzania. Otherwise they would come under obligation to the Tutsis on their own hill, and we might see the confiscation of crops we ourselves had sown.

From what we learned from the old folks, we might even be

compelled to work clearing ground, tending stock, or doing masonry, as in the time of the *mwamis*. Forced, unpaid labor—that could pinch a farmer way beyond reason.

PIO: Maybe we did not hate all the Tutsis, especially our neighbors, and maybe we did not see them as wicked enemies. But among ourselves we said we no longer wanted to live together. We even said we did not want them anywhere around us anymore, and that we had to clear them from our land. It's serious, saying that—it's already sharpening the machete.

Me, I don't know why I started detesting Tutsis. I was young, and what I liked most was soccer: I played on the Kibungo team with Tutsis my own age, we passed the ball around without any hitch. I never noticed any unease in their company. Hatred just showed up at killing time; I latched on to it through imitation, to fit in.

LÉOPORD: It is awkward to talk about hatred between Hutus and Tutsis, because words changed meaning after the killings. Before, we could fool around among ourselves and say we were going to kill them all, and the next moment we would join them to share some work or a bottle. Jokes and threats were mixed together. We no longer paid heed to what we said. We could toss around awful words without awful thoughts. The Tutsis did not even get very upset. I mean, they didn't draw apart because of those unfortunate discussions. Since then we have seen: those words brought on grave consequences.

ALPHONSE: During the dry seasons of early childhood, the Hutu hears grown-ups repeating that Tutsis take up too many plots of land, that we cannot fight poverty in this situation, that those people are too in the way. Then the words are forgotten after abundant harvests. But the child grows used to this grumbling.

Even sitting next to a muddy little Tutsi, a Hutu child feels a natural jealousy of the other child, sees him as a show-off. He gets used to following his parents' lead. Afterward, when a problem arises, he no longer looks it full in the face, he prefers to glare at the Tutsi who just happens to be passing by.

PANCRACE: The radios were yammering at us since 1992 to kill all the Tutsis; there was anger after the president's death and a fear of falling under the rule of the *inkotanyi*. But I do not see any hatred in all that.

The Hutu always suspects that some plans are cooking deep in the Tutsi character, nourished in secret since the passing of the ancien régime. He sees a threat lurking in even the feeblest or kindest Tutsi. But it is suspicion, not hatred. The hatred came over us suddenly after our president's plane crashed. The intimidators shouted, "Just look at these cockroaches—we told you so!" And we yelled, "Right, let's go hunting!" We weren't that angry; more than anything else, we were relieved.

IGNACE: I do not know if killing Tutsis is different from killing non-Tutsis, since we have no experience of that. In Rwanda, if we don't meet a brother Hutu, we meet a Tutsi, since the Twa pygmies are invisible in their forests and the whites are white. In harmony, in discord, it is impossible for us to encounter ordinary people, like us, who are not Tutsi. What I mean is, in private killings or bigger ones, all we know is killing Tutsis.

ÉLIE: In the cities, many Hutus envied the Tutsi women they could not have, because of their tall, slim figures, their polished features, and their fashionable ways of serving family meals or dressing for ceremonies. And yet on the hills, the Hutus could see for themselves that the women all grew weary together out in the fields. I don't know of any farmer who went to ask for a tall girl from a Tutsi neighbor for his son, so I don't know of anyone who was refused.

The cows and the land are what came before the jealousies about looks. Especially the cows, because the Tutsis had the habit of herding them together so you couldn't count anymore which were whose. They never wanted to admit how many they owned—not to their wives, or their sons, or the authorities. Us, we would see the herds going by, hidden in the thickets, tended by cowherds in rags, and it would eat at us. On the hills, secrets about possessions are dangerous.

ADALBERT: There are people like me who bad-mouthed the Tutsis easily. We repeated what we had been hearing for a long time. We called them arrogant, fussy, even spiteful. But we saw no such arrogance or haughty manners when we were together in the choir or at the market. Not even in the *cabarets* or on the banana plantations if a help-out came up.

The oldsters all had a hand in muddling things between us, but they did it in good faith, so to speak. Afterward the radios exaggerated to get us all fired up. "Cockroaches," "snakes"—it was the radios that taught us those words. The evil-mindedness of the radios was too well calculated for us to oppose it.

ALPHONSE: As to the Tutsis' fancy manners, I believe that in the end we were used to them. It was all the same to us, that gossip about dainty fingers and peculiarities of the sort. I do not believe the cows presented a truly hateful problem, or else we could just have slaughtered cows. I do not believe our hearts detested the

Tutsis. But it was inevitable to think so, since the decision was made by the organizers to kill them all.

To kill so many human beings without wavering, we had to hate with no second thoughts. Hatred was the only emotion allowed for the Tutsis. The killings were too well managed to leave us room for any other feelings.

AN UNNATURAL SLAUGHTER

Contemporary Africa has been the theater for a genocide, and a great many Africans find it hard to understand or accept this. It will take a long time for them to come to terms with such a reality, just as it took an inordinately long time for Europeans and Americans to come to terms with the Jewish genocide.

Even more Africans deny the African origin of the Rwandan genocide, arguing that it is a tragedy fomented elsewhere, as Berthe claims: "The case of Rwanda goes beyond African customs. An African massacres from anger or hunger in the belly. Or he slaughters just enough to seize diamonds or a suchlike prize. He does not massacre with a full belly and a peaceful heart on hills covered with bean fields, like the *interahamwe*, who I believe mislearned a lesson from elsewhere, outside of Africa. I do not know who planted the idea of the genocide. No, I am not saying it was the colonists. Truly I do not know who, but it was not an African."

Here, however, her judicious, generous, and open-minded intelligence fails her through lack of historical perspective. All genocides go beyond customs, be they European, American, Asian, or African. And those who thought that Africa's wealth of flourishing cultures, ancestral wisdom, permissive traditions, and appetite for life would protect it from the danger of genocide were wrong.

I could use this comment about the universality of genocide to update some age-old questions: in the place of Pio, Fulgence,

Pancrace, and the others in the gang, what would Europeans or Americans have done? What would we have dared to do, or refused to do? What would have happened to us? But there is no point to those questions, not so much because we cannot get inside the skin of bean farmers on a hill in Rwanda, but because we cannot imagine being born and growing up under such a despotic, ethnocentric regime, and because outside of a few individuals secure in their courage and moral strength, most of us would come up with something like, "We would have slacked off, lagged far behind the group, and not dirtied our machetes"—privately hoping for better, without dispelling an iota of doubt.

Instead, let us replace the questions with a few observations. In postwar Germany, throughout forty years of trials of Nazi criminals, not one defense lawyer could cite a single case of a German who was severely punished for refusing to kill an unarmed Gypsy or Jew. During the operations of that 101st Battalion of police reservists, according to Christopher Browning, not one policeman was punished for refusing to shoot. (He estimates that 80 to 90 percent of the five hundred reservists did follow orders.)

In Rwanda the massacres were over too quickly for the administration implementing the genocide to hold trials and condemn anyone who refused to kill. True, tens of thousands of Hutus were murdered because of their moral objections to the slaughter, but no examples have surfaced of someone arrested simply for refusing to kill, except in very specific cases: spouses in mixed marriages or people accused of having hidden Tutsis. In Kibungo, Ntarama, Kanzenze, and throughout the commune of Nyamata, anyone who publicly opposed the genocide, by word or deed, risked being executed or condemned to kill a victim on the spot. Everybody had to participate in some way, to be involved in the killings, destruction, and looting, or to contribute monetarily. Still, I repeat: no one was seriously threatened with physical harm for reluctance to use a machete on a Tutsi. And though it was possible to "resist" through auxiliary activities, exceptions, and simple shirking, the estimates of the number of killers in Nyamata are almost beyond belief.

Christine, daughter of a Tutsi father and a Hutu mother, tries to explain it this way: "I think someone who was forced to kill wanted his neighbors to have to kill, too, so they would all be considered the same. Compared to your neighbor who killed every day, you could seem lazy or recalcitrant and a really bad helper, but you did have to show yourself worthy by reddening your hands that one time."

To understand the voluntary service of the thugs of the Third Reich, which was often most astounding *outside* Germany, historians and philosophers make much of the formidable discipline that a totalitarian state can impose upon its citizens; the effectiveness of constant and insidious propaganda; and above all, the power of social conformity in situations of fear and crisis (not to be confused with conditions during a war, which on the contrary can sometimes completely destroy social cohesion and conformity). But these arguments are not enough to explain the killing machine described by Christine. At some time in their history, Russians, Spaniards, Argentines, Romanians, Iraqis, and many other peoples have experienced the efficiency of machines designed to destroy the human spirit—machinery created by Stalin, Franco, Videla, Ceauşescu, Hussein, dictators who gained from their populations massive submission, renunciation, a kind of debasement, and a tolerance for denunciation, but who never raised enthusiastic processions of ordinary people who every day went singing off to work as killers.

If historians and philosophers were to gloss over the exceptional, irrational nature of genocide, they would risk appearing ambiguous, even hurtful insofar as they might encourage pessimism and bigotry or, worse, spread the foulest social plague of all: cynicism. The simplest definition of this exceptional nature of genocide comes from Jean-Baptiste Munyankore, a teacher in Ntarama for forty-three years: "The things that happened in Nyamata, in the churches, in the marshes, and on the hills, were the abnormal actions of perfectly normal people."

Or from Sylvie, who observes, "If you linger too long in fear of genocide, you lose hope. You lose what you have managed to salvage from life. You risk contamination from a different madness. When I think about the genocide, in moments of calm, I mull over where to put it properly away in life, but I find no place. I simply mean to say, it is no longer anything human."

WORDS TO AVOID SAYING IT

FULGENCE: The more we saw people die, the less we thought about their lives, the less we talked about their deaths. And the more we got used to enjoying it. And the more we told ourselves, deep inside, that since we knew how to do it, we really should do it down to the very last one. This final viewpoint seemed natural amid the uproar and the shouting, but it went without saying.

ALPHONSE: We slogged through the marshes with a crowd of people to kill. The mud came up to our ankles, sometimes to our knees. The sun hammered our skulls. The papyrus tore our shirts and the skin beneath. Colleagues were watching us. If they saw trembling, they sneered and called us cowards. If they saw hesitation, they grew angry and accused us of treachery. If they saw generosity, they scolded and called us old women. They were quick to abuse us.

In that situation, the jeering of colleagues is awful to overcome if it gets around your neighborhood. It is just the same in school or in the *cabaret*, but more serious in the marshes. This taunting is a poison in life. You try to protect yourself from it, of course. So you join the camp of the ones doing it. When the killings begin, you find it easier to ply the machete than to be stabbed by ridicule and contempt. This truth is impossible to understand for anyone who was not there beside us.

That is what I want to say. In the tumult of killings, stepping aside is not viable for a person, since that person would then find only his neighbors' backs to talk to about ordinary concerns. Being alone is too risky for us. So the person jumps up at the signal and takes part, even if the price is the bloody work you know.

ÉLIE: Ever since independence, the intimidators were always fiddling around with the idea of killing, taking care never to say it outright. For example, when they announced, "There's not enough land in this country for two ethnic groups, and neither one will leave, so it is up to the Hutus to solve the problem," that meant what could not be said.

The intimidators did not want any trouble, above all from pointless talk about what they were up to. We felt there wouldn't be anything left to talk about when it was over and done with. Basically, we agreed to go for it without speaking of it. What we were doing seemed less unnatural to us if we didn't have to say it. And there are still words we do not want to pronounce, even among colleagues.

PANCRACE: Killings of that kind are hungry for death, not for life, as with wild animals. Such killings feed on everyone they see, they are never satisfied; as long as there is still someone left, they spur you on until the last of the last. That is why they do without words. Except for ridiculous words, obviously. On the radio we'd hear that the *inkotanyi* had tails or pointy ears; even if no one believed it, it did us good to hear it. Those were not very nice jokes, but we laughed anyway. It was better than hearing nothing at all.

ÉLIE: No one can admit the whole sad truth, not now, not ever. No one can speak all the precise words of his misdeeds without damning himself in other people's eyes. And that's too grim. But without fear of seeming more punishable, a small number are beginning to recount some ugly bits and pieces, to do penance for the blood they splattered. Those few are clearing a path of sincerity. It is a big thing.

On the hills or in prison, truth offers every participant a share. The survivors have the largest share because of what they endured, that's normal. The Tutsi wives who were saved, the international cameramen, the soldiers have shares. But if the offenders' share is missing, the revelations about those killings will go around in circles forever. The offenders know more than the basic facts they remember, more than the details about how things were managed. They have secrets in their souls.

JEAN-BAPTISTE: The whole time the killings went on, I never heard the word *genocide*. It reached our ears only through the voices of international reporters and humanitarian officials, first on the road into exile—but we did not know what the word meant—and then in the camps in Congo.

This is a truth: among ourselves, we never said that word. Many did not even know the meaning of *genocide*. It was of no use. And yet if we were getting up every morning to go hunting, even when we were tired or had other work left unfinished, it was certainly because we thought we had to kill them all. People knew what job they were doing without needing to name it.

ADALBERT: Genocide is not an idea common to wars and battles. It is an idea the authorities have—to rid themselves of a danger once and for all. A convenient idea that need not be named or encouraged, except with the usual malicious outbursts. It's a quite ordinary idea when it flies from word to word, sometimes from joke to joke; it becomes extraordinary when it is caught on the tips of machetes.

This idea does not die with the killings, not after victory, not after defeat. It can be salvaged by future authorities for another destiny. But how can you kill an idea, used so extraordinarily, if you do not know how to kill its word, which can recall it to life? Killing enemies, killing offenders, killing neighbors—that you can understand. Killing ideas and words—that is beyond intelligence, a farmer's intelligence, anyway.

PIO: At the start of a genocide, there is a cause, a reason, and people who find it worthwhile. The cause does not drift around there by accident; it's even fine-tuned by the intimidators: the desire to win the game for good. But the people it tempts are the ones who just happen to live there. And I was there, at home, when the temptation came calling. I'm not saying I was forced by Satan and the like. Through greed and obedience I found the cause worthwhile, and I ran down to the marshes. But if I had been born in Tanzania or in France, I would have been far away from the commotion and dirty bloodshed.

Simple people cannot resist a temptation like that, not without biblical rescue, not on the hills, anyway. Why? Because of the beautiful words of complete success. They win you over. Afterward the temptation cannot go to prison, so they imprison the people. And the temptation can certainly show up just as dreadful further along.

When someone sees what is in his own best interest come right up to him, and his colleagues as well, he loses no more time in waiting and hesitation, he no longer considers feelings, no longer hears pleas for mercy. He sees Evil in the form of Good and is content with it. He thinks of all he will gain for himself and his family until the end of his days. He follows his own best interest into the swamps.

Afterward he cleans himself of filthy mud and blood the way

he downs a Primus. That is what I did. I'm not saying I am not at fault. But I am punished both for my mistake and for my unlucky fate.

IGNACE: It was kill or be killed. Each morning there were those who had to die and those who had to kill. Anyone who spoke out against the killings was killed, even for a murmur. Anyone who slipped away slowed down the killings of his colleagues, and he had to hide until he was found out and penalized. In the end, what you call genocide is killings that offer only one option.

ADALBERT: Agriculture is something you cannot hurry; it follows its seasons. The killings, on the contrary, they followed our whims. You want more, you strike more, you shed more blood, you take more. And what is more—if it's a genocide, you know you will take everything for good, except for the quarreling, the transgressions, and all those other bad words you leave behind in the arms of death.

LÉOPORD: I can give you endless details about the killings. But when you ask me to tell you my thoughts during those awkward moments . . . I don't know what to reply.

The killings were very well arranged, they seemed profitable to us. We were obedient and encouraged in a propitious new situation. We started, we got used to it, we were satisfied. The farmer going down to his field wonders along the way whether he should plant beans or corn. The teacher going to his school debates which lesson he will pull out for his class. The mechanic chooses the engine part he is going to clean. But the killer in the marshes is not bothered by personal questions. He puts great effort into his work. He follows his colleagues and chases his victims. He counts his riches. Many of our thoughts were empty, and they left no memories behind.

IGNACE: We called them "cockroaches," an insect that chews up clothing and nests in it, so you have to squash them hard to get rid of them. We didn't want any more Tutsis on the land. We imagined an existence without them. At first, we favored getting rid of them without actually killing them. If they had agreed to leave—for Burundi or other likely destinations—they could have gone and saved their lives. And we wouldn't have piled up the fatalities of the massacres. But they couldn't imagine living there without their ancient traditions and their herds of cows. That pushed us toward the machetes.

The Tutsis had accepted so many killings without ever protesting, they had waited for death or bad blows so often without raising their voices, that in a certain way we thought deep down they were fated to die, here and now, all together. We thought that since this job was meeting no opposition, it was because it really had to be done. That idea helped us not to think about the job. Afterward we learned what it was called. But among us here in prison, we don't use that word.

JEAN-BAPTISTE: After the plane crash, we talked from group to group about wiping out the Tutsis. But to me, the words didn't ring true, I was thinking only about doing some killing soon. The evening of the massacre in the church, the seriousness of it overturned everything: I understood that words and deeds had come together. The deeds now promised to be definitive, and the words useless.

You could feel uneasy about the activity waiting for you in the marshes. But you whispered, This job is going to be completely finished, and if I don't contribute my share, I will seem a defeatist afterward, and that's too penalizing. So you followed close on your colleagues' heels, you did it without a word, and after a while you got used to it and you joked around like before. But speaking true words about that situation, that is risky no matter what.

Jean: "For a little boy who zigzagged among those bloody ambushes, there is nothing to be gained by speaking of it one way or another. The words he will use about what he did will play a mean trick on him, in his mind or someone else's. The lower his age and the higher his voice at the time of the killings, the more serious his words have become. People will say of him, This boy has seen too deep an evil; he will denounce a transgressor; he has dirtied his arm where he should not have gone; and what he is saying will torment those around him. He will not make a proper adult, so from now on he must stay one step aside.

"Therefore, truly, silence alone can help him."

FULGENCE: That massacre, we did not speak of it beforehand because it was the business of the intimidators and was being prepared outside of earshot. We did not speak of it during, since there were better things to do. And now they tell us we have to speak of everything. Of what, since we are the last ones to have to talk about it? Of what we saw? Why us, since everyone saw the same thing? Why not ask our compatriots who stand around gaping at their banana trees in blissful contemplation? Tell what we did in detail? What use is that, except to be even more penalized? Tell the why of it? What for, since we never found out what was being schemed on the sly?

Most amazing of all is that no one ever bothered to explain

the why of our killings to us properly beforehand, and no one is going to do it now. Except to count off years of prison for us.

Clémentine: "The wives of the killers never talk about the genocide. They never mention this word among themselves. It no more exists than the repentance that goes with it. These women say they regret the absence of their men, the poverty that awaits them each morning, and the bad words that have spread throughout the region—as if these things were natural calamities.

"They pray, they sing, they deny, and not only because they are afraid. They feel more furious than guilty. They are more miserable over the unkept promises of their husbands than over the complaints and accusations of the survivors. They keep silent, swindled on all sides."

PIO: Killing Tutsis . . . I never even thought about it when we lived in neighborly harmony. Even pushing and shoving or trading harsh words didn't seem right to me. But when everyone began getting out their machetes at the same time, I did so too, without delay. I had only to do as my colleagues did and think of the advantages. Especially since we knew they were going to leave the world of the living for all time.

When you receive firm orders, promises of long-term benefits, and you feel well backed up by colleagues, the wickedness of killing until your arm falls off is all one to you. I mean, you naturally feel pulled along by all those opinions and their fine words.

A genocide—that seems extraordinary to someone who arrives afterward, like you, but for someone who got himself muddled up by the intimidators' big words and the joyful shouts of his colleagues, it seemed like a normal activity.

LÉOPORD: When the Tutsis were caught, many died without a word. In Rwanda people say "die like a lamb in the Bible." Of course in Rwanda there are no sheep, so we have never heard their cry.

It sometimes touched us painfully that they awaited death in silence. Evenings, we would ask over and over, "Why no protest from these people who are about to leave? Why do they not beg for mercy?"

The organizers claimed that the Tutsis felt guilty for the sin of being Tutsi. Some *interahamwe* kept saying they felt responsible for the misfortunes they had brought upon us.

Well, I knew that was not true. The Tutsis were not asking for anything in those fatal moments because they no longer believed in words. They had no more faith in crying out, like frightened animals, for example, howling to be heard above the mortal blows. An overpowering sorrow was carrying those people away. They felt so abandoned they did not even open their mouths.

DEATH IN THE EYE
OF A KILLER

We are driving through the immense and flourishing forest of Nyungwe in western Rwanda. It's an August morning in 1994, and the only road into this area is jammed with an endless column of Hutus fleeing from the cities of Butare and Gikongoro toward the border town of Cyangugu. There they will gather to cross the river lying between them and the camps of Congo.

A few kilometers back, some forest rangers told us that rather than go farther into exile, tens of thousands of Hutu refugees have scattered deep into the woods, preferring to shelter in huts of branches and live in the old way, hunting and gathering. Out of curiosity, we turn off the paved road onto a path and enter a half-light troubled only by the deep notes of yellow-beaked cuckoos, their clamor answered by the vibrant cries of warblers.

In a clearing at the end of the path, we come upon about a dozen men crouching around a fire as rising coils of smoke melt into the mist. Sabou, the interpreter who has been with me for weeks now, alerts me immediately: "Watch out, they are *interahamwe*." Sabou is neither Hutu nor Tutsi, but a young Congolese from the nearby city of Bukavu who speaks fluent Kinyarwanda. I don't understand his warning at first, thinking he means "Hutus," which seems obvious, but what he is thinking is, "killers."

The men wear ragged shorts or pants and most of them are shirtless. Some have fashioned garments of leaves for camouflage or protection from downpours. Under their watchful eye, colobus monkeys brought down by their arrows are roasting on spits, their black and white skins tossed aside. Bows and machetes lie next to the men, but no firearms, no baggage.

The men greet us politely, inviting us to sit down and wait for some roast meat. They ask us about the situation at the border. We chat warily about their journey from home and their life as hunters but never about their previous activities, naturally. Sabou, ordinarily an exuberant soul, remains noticeably subdued.

Suddenly, several of the men rise, machetes in hand, and surround us. The atmosphere has changed completely without my realizing it. Thanks to the sixth sense and sangfroid of Sabou, who has anticipated the confrontation and keeps talking to the men, we manage to retreat, slowly and carefully, and to get inside our car before the first blows rain down. We back away at top speed as the men slam their machetes on the the car, furious to see their prizes escape: car, clothes, money, and a sack of bananas.

The scene took enough time—or seemed "slowed down" enough—for us to observe its berserk violence in detail. Afterward we could remember everything about those faces grotesquely frozen in hatred, and those shouts, those eyes alight with madness and death.

People who travel through war zones tell us that the gaze of someone who is about to kill lodges more deeply in the memory than a death itself, and that they have been more shocked by scenes of execution—even when faked—than by the carnage during attacks and bombardments.

Those men in the clearing were not from the Bugesera, but they might just as well have been. Yet during my visits to Rilima, the faces of the men from Kibungo have never shown the slightest sign that might recall that explosive scene. I mention it here because I wonder now if, unconsciously, I didn't go to the penitentiary, among other reasons, expecting to find those same expressions of unfathomable hatred, to compare them to my memories and establish a link with the past. Whatever the nature of my action, I believe I went to Rilima above all to see the killers, the fathers and brothers of those mute and mistrustful Hutus stubbornly holed up on their plots of land—and to talk with them, if possible, even if it meant raising questions in the minds of readers of this book.

For example, is it ethical, not to talk to such killers, but to encourage them to speak for themselves? More to the point: is it ethical to publish interviews with prisoners who have been deprived of their physical liberty and thus of freedom of expression?

At other times, in other countries, I have met people incarcerated because of war: enemy prisoners, individuals suspected of treason, of collaboration, of crime, of rape, or those born into the wrong ethnic group or with the wrong name. I have heard a great many "compromised" conversations or confessions. I have systematically refused to publish accounts of them or sometimes—such was the pressure exerted by the jailers—even to listen to them, so as not to be a party to the prisoners' humiliation.

So why did I make an exception in Nyamata? Offhand, I can list many reasons, among them the complete indifference of the prison authorities in Rilima, which ensured their discretion during and after our visits; the strong bonds, sometimes of friendship, which I continue to enjoy with the survivors; the unbearable, intolerable silence of the Hutus I have met outside the prison and the gloomy unease that weighs on the hills; the specific character of the genocide, which belies every preconception you may have about it; and the power of Hannah Arendt's *Eichmann in Jerusalem*, which was written after she had listened to the words of a prisoner—indeed, on the eve of his sentencing.

The most honest answer is that perhaps I became swept up in the project, that the whole question simply faded away during the interviews, and that when I returned to Paris the question no longer worried me, for it was immediately replaced by other, more pressing ones.

A leader of killers on the hill of Kibungo, of refugees in the Congolese camp, and of a security force and a choral group in prison, Adalbert is the one with whom the interviews must begin. The first day he sits down on the bench, full of energy, and at the opening question starts talking about a battle. The Tutsis against the Hutus: attacks all over the place, advances, retreats, flanking movements by men with machetes, reinforcements armed with guns on the opposite flank, heroic fighting to hold a strategic house, fields abandoned during the struggle . . .

We listen to him incredulously; Innocent grows ever more frustrated, while I try to guess what Adalbert is up to. When I tell him he can't fob that nonsense off on me because I have visited Rwanda many times since the genocide, Adalbert shows no disappointment or irritation, but in reply to a new question, he simply picks up his epic right where he left off.

Does he want to show hostility to the book project? Is he making sport of us? Not in the least. Is he relating what he wishes to be his truth, not giving a hoot what we think? Perhaps, but there's more to it than that. When doubt eats away at him, perhaps he creates an imaginary world into which he escapes alone or with his pals. Two weeks pass before he begins talking more realistically.

The next person to take his seat beneath the acacia branches is Alphonse, who launches without hesitation into a description of his first killing spree. He is precise as to gestures, dialogue, facts, deeds. But he talks with the ready fluency of a sportsman returning from a turkey shoot. His bonhomie and the wealth of details he gives us are as intriguing as Adalbert's flights of fancy.

As for Fulgence, he pauses constantly, sometimes in the middle of a phrase, looking from side to side as if each question were bringing him to a crossroads with no signpost . . .

In fact all of them, each in his own way, behave bizarrely during their initial sessions, as though they were emerging from some sort of imaginary bubble.

The episodes that turned their lives upside down might well explain their retreat into this bubble. After all, these men had seemed destined for nothing beyond choosing a wife to share a rural existence on a hill in a little country in the heart of Africa, a life lived in uneasy tolerance of their neighbors, without television or any influx of immigration to connect them to the vast outside world. From one day to the next, they let themselves be swept up in a whirlwind of phenomenal carnage; then their first trip took place in a panicked exodus of two million compatriots, and their first visit abroad was to refugee camps where they remained for more than two years with no prospects for the future. Finally, without even seeing their homes again, some of them were thrown into prison with seven thousand confederates and no link to the outside world except radio.

Yet the serenity they display places them at such a level of unreality and aberration that it cannot be attributed solely to the violent upheavals of their lives, or to the walls that protect them, shielding them from accusing eyes as well as from the alcoholism, mistrust, and fear that reign over their three hills. Not one of them presents the slightest symptom of psychic distress. Not one of them shows signs of any disturbance, and to hear them tell it, barely a dozen prisoners in all are psychologically troubled. There are regrets, complaints, homesickness, dejection, and ailments due to imprisonment—but never any fits of depression about their machete blows.

Meeting them again in the penitentiary six years after knowing them in Kibungo, Innocent says, "I thought they had become bitter, miserable, savage, and I am just astonished now to see them sometimes smiling and youthful. They seem more like boarders than prisoners. What's more, they speak of the genocide as of a barbarity already long past, a thing simply ordered up by the authorities." At every interview, the men speak in even voices with a familiar tone that denotes astonishing impassiveness.

If the ferocity glimpsed in the forest of Nyungwe had ever surfaced in any of their faces, would we have stopped the interview? I really don't know. On the other hand, their unshakable placidity is clearly quite important in the interviews—both smoothing over boredom and disgust, and raising nagging questions. Why are these guys participating in this project? Why are they agreeing to speak to us, often quite frankly, sometimes even with striking naïveté? Or rather, why do they say what they say without any mea culpas or remorse (whether sincere or not) and without expecting compensation? These unanswered questions keep us on our toes and encourage us to bear with the unbearable moments.

Still, if I had to pick out the most impressive facet of the men's personalities on display, it would be not their calm detachment but their egocentrism, almost equally overpowering in all of them, at times just unbelievable. When they talk about the genocide, they are not describing an event in which they were simply peripheral figures; they place themselves at the center of a swirl of activity involving victims, survivors, officials, priests, *interahamwe*, whites,* and so on. The paradox is that while they minimize their participation and shift the blame onto others (the Hutu government, the *interahamwe*, possibly even whites and Tutsis), at the same time they focus only on themselves in the story, then and now.

They do not all interpret the killings in the same way. Although Élie, Alphonse, and Léopord would like to understand the events better, Pio and Pancrace admit that they are beyond their comprehension, while Jean-Baptiste seems to sense the monstrosity of their actions and their effect on the world. Obsessed as they are with finding a safe way out, Adalbert, Ignace, and Joseph-Désiré constantly trip themselves up while making a show of soul-searching.

These differences notwithstanding—which provoke no shouting matches because the men never discuss such things among themselves—the killers worry only about their own fates and essentially feel no compassion for anyone but themselves. Some of them, evaluating the catastrophic results of that bloody episode, catalogue its effects on their blighted future. When we tackle the theme of regret, not one of them spontaneously mentions the victims. They think of them, but only afterward: their instinctive reaction is to dwell on their own personal losses and hardships. One day Fulgence says, "We saw the first awful consequences of the killings on our way to Congo, with the moaning of our starving bellies and the terrible rumblings of turmoil at our heels." Their natural tendency to dwell on their own suffering is stupefying.

Unlike war criminals, who tend (aside from certain psychopaths) to lie low and slip out the back door after their down-

---

Whom they often call muzungu, which means "he who has taken the place."

fall, these fellows usually place themselves in the center of the stage.

I have only one tentative explanation for this unusual behavior. The absolute character of their project was what allowed them to carry it out with a certain equanimity, and today this same absoluteness allows them to avoid fully understanding and agonizing over what they did. The monstrous nature of the extermination haunts the survivors and even tortures them with guilt, whereas it exculpates and reassures the killers, perhaps protecting them from madness.

We meet every morning on the main street. Innocent, a much earlier riser, gossips with Marie-Louise as he waits on a bench in front of her shop, sometimes with a bottle of Primus already between his knees. Although he's not fond of sweet things, I often take him across the street to the veranda of Sylvie's *boulangerie-pâtisserie*. We start our day with milky tea and freshly baked doughnuts while we crack jokes about the owner's mood swings. Then I make the rounds of the pharmacies with a sheaf of prescriptions signed by the director of the prison infirmary. The kindness of the women pharmacists and the ritual of these purchases for the gang members make this a pleasant chore, like the idea of seeing them again, as we roll along on our way to the prison.

At first, I feel only natural hatred or aversion for them; at best, in a few instances, condescension. I do not need either the "feedback" of Innocent's highly reactive presence or contact with my daily circle of Marie-Louise, Sylvie and her clients, Édith and her children, Claudine, and all my Tutsi friends on the hills to keep me from falling into a syndrome of indulgent complacency.

But as time goes by, a kind of perplexity creeps in, which makes the Kibungo gang not more likable but less unpleasant to spend time with—under the acacia tree, anyway. This is awkward to admit, but curiosity wins out over hostility.

Their friendly solidarity, their disconnection from the world they soaked in blood, their incomprehension of their new existence, their inability to notice how we see them—all this makes them more accessible. Their patience and serenity, and sometimes their naïveté, finally rub off on our relationship and touch particularly on their mysterious willingness to talk. They don't give a hang about bearing witness for history; they have no complexes to work off and no hopes for any clemency from these pages. They are probably opening up because for the first time they can do so without feeling threatened.

But there is more to it than that. Some of them occasionally reveal that they no longer completely recognize themselves in those men who marched down to the marshes, singing, and others seem to fear what they became there. Perhaps their egocentrism is less egotistic than it seems. Perhaps they harbor more self-doubt than their accounts would lead us to believe. Perhaps they feel the need to glimpse themselves as they were, even from this distance, in the stories they tell. Perhaps they are telling their stories to convince us they are ordinary, the ordinary people described by Primo Levi and Hannah Arendt. In some confused way they are also probably trying to emphasize, to all of us at the edge of that exterminating whirlwind, an agonizing truth.

ALPHONSE: Some offenders claim that we changed into wild animals, that we were blinded by ferocity, that we buried our civilization under branches, and that's why we are unable to find the right words to talk properly about it.

That is a trick to sidetrack the truth. I can say this: outside the marshes, our lives seemed quite ordinary. We sang on the paths, we downed Primus or *urwagwa*, we had our choice amid abundance. We chatted about our good fortune, we soaped off our bloodstains in the basin, and our noses enjoyed the aromas of full cooking pots. We rejoiced in the new life about to begin by feasting on leg of veal. We were hot at night atop our wives, and we scolded our rowdy children. Although no longer willing to feel pity, we were still greedy for good feelings.

The days all seemed much alike, as I told you. We put on our field clothes. We swapped gossip at the *cabaret*, we made bets on our victims, spoke mockingly of cut girls, squabbled foolishly over looted grain. We sharpened our tools on whetting stones. We traded stories about desperate Tutsi tricks, we made fun of every "Mercy!" cried by someone who'd been hunted down, we counted up and stashed away our goods.

We went about all sorts of human business without a care in the world—provided we concentrated on killing during the day, naturally.

At the end of that season in the marshes, we were so disappointed we had failed. We were disheartened by what we were going to lose, and truly frightened by the misfortune and vengeance reaching out for us. But deep down, we were not tired of anything.

WRITTEN IN MARCH 2003

THE KILLERS

When the interviews were over, I suggested to the gang that we take a photograph of them. I told them it would be published, so that readers could attach faces to their accounts. I thought the men would have reservations, but they readily agreed, except for Adalbert, who refused even to discuss it and was absent on the day the picture was taken. The photo shows them on the benches in the garden where my interviews took place. It's like one of those commemorative photographs celebrating a departure or the end of something.

From left to right: Joseph-Désiré, Léopord, Élie, Fulgence, Pio, Alphonse, Jean-Baptiste, Ignace, and Pancrace.

JOSEPH-DÉSIRÉ BITERO

He was born on the hill of Kanazi to parents who were farmers, and at the time of the killings he was thirty-one years old. As a cousin of the burgomaster, he had joined the MRND, President Habyarimana's party, at an early age. He is married and the father of two children who live on the family farmland. A graduate of a teachers' training college, he taught and lived in Nyamata. He was in charge of the MRND party's youth movement and in 1993 was named municipal president of the *interahamwe*, the most important Hutu extremist militia.

As such, he is the only member of the gang to have been implicated in the preparation of the genocide several months before it began. After his conviction, his house in the Gatare neighborhood in Nyamata was confiscated to pay his fines. His wife was not prosecuted, but she has not been able to return to her job at the Sainte-Marthe Maternity Hospital. With her two daughters, she returned to live in a family house in Kanazi to cultivate their fields there.

Accused of crimes of genocide and crimes against humanity with premeditation, Joseph-Désiré was prosecuted individually at a trial in the municipal court of Nyamata that was very closely followed. The court rejected his superficial and contradictory confessions for their lack of sincerity, and he was condemned to death on July 3, 1998. His appeal of the sentence was rejected by the supreme court in Kigali. Because of a delay in his sentencing, he escaped the public execution of April 24, 1998; his probable fate will be life in prison, at least so long as the current régime of President Paul Kagame remains in power.

LÉOPORD TWAGIRAYEZU

He was born in Muyange, on the hill of Maranyundo. He was twenty-two at the time of the killings, a son of farmers, like all the others in the gang. He has four sisters. He attended elementary school, then worked in the family fields. Like Joseph-Désiré Bitero, he was a member of the MRND, but only for two years, and he had no real responsibilities. He has been a fervent Catholic since childhood.

Accused of crimes of genocide and crimes against humanity, he pleaded guilty to numerous murders and acts committed in his capacity as a cell leader. In 2001 the municipal court in Nyamata sentenced him to seven years in prison. The importance of his confession and the effectiveness of his cooperation with the police and judicial authorities during the preliminary investigation of his case explain why his sentence was lighter than those of his companions. He did not appeal it.

He served almost all of his sentence (having been in prison since 1995) and was released in December 2002 without being sent on to a reeducation camp. His neighbors greeted him with insults and threats during an official ceremony of forgiveness, however, and he has not yet returned to his home on the hill of Maranyundo.

ÉLIE MIZINGE

He was born in Gisenyi, in western Rwanda, near the Congolese border. Fifty years old at the time of the killings, he was quite familiar with the ancien régime, since he was fourteen at the death of the last Tutsi king, before independence. A soldier, he arrived in the Bugesera in 1974 to invest his savings in land and found a suitable plot in Karambo, on the hill of Muyenzi. He left the army, joined the municipal police force, then hung up his uniform to become a farmer in 1992, when he was more or less dismissed in the aftermath of a murder. He is married; two of his three children are dead.

The preliminary investigation of his case is over, but he was not tried with his friends, doubtless because of his past career as a soldier and policeman. He will probably be brought up before a *gaçaça,*★ a people's court, and will likely be sentenced at most to two or three years of community service, which means probation, plus three days of unpaid work each week in a private business or government office. For now he is in the camp at Bicumbi, where he attends civics classes with his comrades. Upon his release, he will await his trial at home, not in prison.

FULGENCE BUNANI

He was born in the Gitarama region, and like all his pals in the gang, he is the son of farmers. Thirty-three years old at the time of the killings, he was thirty-nine when the interviews began. After completing elementary school, he became a farmer in Kiganwa, on the hill of Kibungo. A fervent Catholic, he served as a voluntary deacon during lesser rites in the church in Kibungo and filled in for the priest, who had to minister to several parishes. Fulgence's wife and two young children live on their plot of land.

Fulgence was one of some forty prisoners tried by the municipal court of Nyamata, which sits in a building near the penitentiary, far from the hills and the town itself. Accused of crimes of genocide and crimes against humanity, he pleaded guilty to aiding and abet-

---

★*Literally, "the flattened grass under the elders' tree"; a tribal court that renders traditional justice. Faced with the collapse of its judiciary due to the death, flight, or complicity of so many judges during the genocide, the Rwandan government reactivated the gaçaças to speed up the trials of persons suspected of participation in the genocide and to involve Rwandan citizens in the collective work of assigning and admitting individual responsibility for the massacres. At the level of the hills and towns, the gaçaça arraigns the accused in the community where the crime took place, and the local population gives testimony or passes judgment under the supervision of more or less professional officers. This judicial undertaking began in the spring of 2002, and the many assemblies have produced controversial results.*

People accused of genocide have been classified according to four categories of severity; those in the first category (ideologues, propagandists, high-ranking leaders, rapists, and well-known killers) may not be judged by gaçaças.

ting murder. The court accepted his plea and on March 29, 2002, sentenced him to twelve years in the Rilima penitentiary. He did not appeal the sentence to the supreme court in Kigali. Following the presidential decree of January 1, 2003, intended to diminish the prison population drastically, he was released on January 21 after six years in prison and placed for four months in a reeducation camp in Bicumbi, in northeastern Nyamata. He was released on probation on May 5, 2003, and went home to Kiganwa.

PIO MUTUNGIREHE

He was born in Nyarunazi, on the hill of Kibungo. Twenty years old at the time of the killings, he is unmarried, from a family of four brothers and sisters. He played on the "mixed" soccer team of Kibungo, was a fan of the Bugesera Sports soccer team, and was a dedicated member of the Kibungo Choral Society. After finishing elementary school, he worked in the family fields located between Nyarunazi and Kiganwa.

He was tried along with Fulgence, Pancrace, and Adalbert. He pleaded guilty to certain murders and on March 29, 2002, was sentenced to the same punishment as his friends: twelve years in prison. He did not appeal the sentence. He too was sent to the reeducation camp in Bicumbi for four months and, like the others, was released on May 5, 2003, free and exempt from any community labor, like all those in the gang aside from Élie and Alphonse.

In tiptop shape, he is eager to take up soccer again.

ALPHONSE HITIYAREMYE

He was born in the province of Kibuye, west of Nyamata. In 1977 he was brought to the Bugesera as a hired field worker by a Tutsi landowner. He later bought his own plot of land in Nyamabuye, between the hills of Kanzenze and Kibungo. He also owned a business in Kanzenze that did well—he has a good head for such things. He was thirty-nine the year of the killings. Married, he is the father of four children. He was a good soccer player and a good Catholic. His wife lives and works on their plot of land.

His judicial situation is unusual. The preliminary investigation of his case was closed, but for no apparent reason he was not one of the forty defendants at the trial of Fulgence, Adalbert, Pio, and the others. He was released on May 5, 2003, but will doubtless be tried by a *gaçaça* court. Like Élie, he thus risks being sentenced to several years of probation involving community labor. Such jobs may run the gamut from working as a doctor in a dispensary to toiling on a road gang.

JEAN-BAPTISTE MURANGIRA

He was born near Gikongoro, in central Rwanda. He was thirty-eight at the time of the killings. After completing his secondary schooling, he obtained a good civil service position as a census taker and local official, but after losing his jobs, he returned to farming. He is married to a Tutsi, Spéciose Mukandahunga, who was spared during the genocide. This marriage is not a sign of tolerance; many officials and prominent citizens wed Tutsi women for reasons of snobbery. His wife still lives in their house and cultivates their plot of land in Rugunga, a hamlet of Tutsis on the hill of Ntarama. He has six children and has had hardly any news of them.

He was the first of the gang to be tried, only a few months after the Hutus had returned from Congo and before the implementation of the policy of national reconciliation, which doubtless explains his relatively severe treatment by the judges. He pleaded guilty to certain murders and was sentenced on

March 30, 1997, to fifteen years in prison. He did not appeal his sentence with the supreme court in Kigali.

He left the Rilima penitentiary in January 2003 after eight years in prison and was sent to the reeducation camp in Bicumbi. At his release on May 5, 2003, he returned home to his Tutsi wife and his land, where he is waiting for a civil service job in Ntarama, Nyamata, or elsewhere.

IGNACE RUKIRAMACUMU

He was born in the area of Gitarama and was sixty-two years old at the time of the killings. Like Élie, he experienced life under the Tutsi monarchy, since he was just shy of thirty when the republic was founded and independence achieved. He arrived in the Bugesera in 1973. After finishing his fourth year of elementary school, he worked as a mason, then acquired a plot of land in Nganwa, on the hill of Kibungo. His wife is dead. Several of his children were killed after the genocide, but he does not have precise information about any of them.

The preliminary investigation of his case is over, and he will not be tried. Following a presidential decree concerning prisoners above the age of seventy, he was released, unconditionally, on January 21, 2003.

He was thus the first member of the gang to be freed. He is back cultivating his fields in Nganwa, is already distilling *urwagwa* again, frequents the Saturday market, and is getting used to a new *cabaret*, since the one he patronized before the killings was destroyed. He talks very little about his recent past.

PANCRACE HAKIZAMUNGILI

He was born in Ruhengeri, on the hill of Kibungo, the year his parents came from Gitarama to the Bugesera. He was twenty-five the year of the killings. By his own admission, his talents run more to chatting with friends in the local *cabaret* than to religion. He is an unmarried farmer with four brothers and sisters. His mother manages the work on the family's land.

Pancrace was among the forty prisoners tried along with Fulgence. He pleaded guilty to certain murders, and his pleas were accepted. He was sentenced the same day as Fulgence to the same punishment: twelve years in prison, a sentence he did not appeal. He too was released from the penitentiary in January 2003, spent four months in the camp at Bicumbi, and became a free man on May 5, 2003.

ADALBERT MUNZIGURA

His parents left Gitarama for the Bugesera in 1970, settling on the hill of Kibungo to begin farming in Ruhengeri, where Adalbert was born. He was twenty-three at the time of the killings. Adalbert is unmarried. Out of his eleven brothers and sisters, the family is sure that seven are still alive. He finished elementary school before going to work in the family fields. He was the choirmaster in Kibungo and a member of the Democratic Republican Movement, a Hutu nationalist party and the MRND's chief rival for power.

Tried along with Fulgence and Pancrace, he pleaded guilty to certain murders. His succinct confession was accepted by the court, to the great displeasure of certain judges and the lawyers of plaintiffs claiming damages. He was sentenced to twelve years in prison. He made no appeal.

On the day of the verdict, the public prosecutor in Nyamata announced that *he* might file an appeal *a minima*, on the grounds that the sentence was too light and failed to reflect the convicted man's responsibilities as the head of a death squad and his active role both before and during the massacres. This prosecutorial appeal was subsequently dropped without explanation.

So Adalbert left the penitentiary at the end of January 2003 for the camp at Bicumbi. On May 5, 2003, he too was released to go home to Ruhengeri, where he was impatiently awaited by his mother, Rose Kubwimana.